THE SEVEN CIRCLES OF DHARMA

Powerful NEW method of Personal Leadership

THE SEVEN CIRCLES OF DHARMA

Powerful NEW method of Personal Leadership

ASHOK THUSSU
ASH TZU

ZORBA BOOKS

ZORBA BOOKS

Published by Zorba Books, January 2023
Website: www.zorbabooks.com
Email: info@zorbabooks.com

Title: **The Seven Circles of Dharma**
Author Name: Ashok Thussu

Printbook ISBN :- 978-93-95217-30-9
Ebook ISBN :- 978-93-95217-31-6

Zorba Books Pvt. Ltd. (opc)
Sushant Arcade,
Next to Courtyard Marriot,
Sushant Lok 1, Gurgaon – 122009, India

Printed in India

This book is dedicated to my parents

Dr. Onkar Nath

Dr. Jagat Mohini

Who spent their lifetime helping others

CONTENTS

PREAMBLE

In India, a commonly used phrase is *Dharam ka Palan Karo.* Literally, this means 'wear' the mantle of righteous behaviour. In a way it also means that action based on positive values is the way to go, and 'wearing' these means exemplifying these in a set of both your intent and deeds, all done fairly.

The exploration in this book on *7CircleDharma* is how to go about exemplifying positive values in your deeds, thus doing the right things as you navigate a complex web of situations, conflicts, circumstances and interactions in life.

I am hugely thankful to many people with whom I had shared the core concept and who encouraged me to put these principles down into writing.

I would like to thank my buddy and colleague Dr. Hiru Bijlani who went through the 1st cut of the manuscript and gave valuable observations and motivation from time to time.

I am also thankful to Prof. Sandeep Mann, who kept reminding me to complete this work and for his encouragement and advice.

My good friend Bharat Wahklu put in a huge effort not only to read the manuscript but also spent time with deeper thought and came up with several suggestions, not all of which I agreed to!

Yet many were valuable as they helped me a lot to get this book into a better flow. Do really appreciate his enthusiastic help and the many conversations we had.

The word Dharma is of Sanskrit origin with the root word Dharan (to wear), the attitude in the context of this book. I may also be using Sanskrit or other words from India but that does not make this work a religious text. This work is independent of any religion and thus can be useful to any person of any faith.

Deepest gratitude and awe for people across successive generations who memorised stories and passed on the knowledge. Even as additional embellishments were added on the secret managed to exist within it all in a hidden form.

Finally, my huge admiration for whoever could weave this construct that I reveal in this work, the *7CircleDharma.* This could be people who thousands of years back had the depth of intellect and clarity of purpose. Many gems get lost, and I am personally delighted to have rediscovered one of their secrets.

There are huge rewards in doing the 'right' things based on the right values and done at the right time. Things you feel you ought to have done but not ended up doing always produces some inner discontent and I hope this book will vastly help you to enhance the quality of your life and the satisfaction you get.

INTRODUCTION

The action one has done cannot be destroyed until it has borne its fruit.

This book is about the practice of Dharma, about doing the 'right' thing. It is not about the exploration of religion or mysterious and deep meaning texts. The *7CircleDharma* represents a very powerful, yet an easy-to-use methodology and, in its own way, defines what practising Dharma is all about - it shows you a robust framework as well as the valuable how-to of practising Dharma in your daily life. It is about a new dimension of Personal Leadership.

So, what exactly is Dharma? It is the consistency of correct behaviour borne out of a balanced, prioritized and done with the correct mindset as we encounter dynamic situations in life. As you think so do you act, and it is these actions that define the word behaviour. We will also delve deep into the meaning and contexts of correct behaviour as we go along. All these have a great bearing on your intent, your thinking constructs and thereafter the actions you do or do not do.

Dharma is a way of living, that moves you through dilemmas and multiple options we encounter in life with clarity and a positive sense of purpose that resonates deeply within you. It is the practice of positive intent and positive yet prioritised actions.

This book has been inspired by stories told of dialogues between Shiva and Parvati at a time when it is said, they observe that someone has died and then Parvati asks and Shiva shares.

(Shiva is a Hindu god described as the destroyer and regenerator of all things. Parvati is his wife and symbolizes, as a goddess, the energy of Shiva.)

Amongst those stories, of rituals and suchlike, lay a theme, hidden and yet strongly present, that led to my discovery of what I share in this *7CircleDharma.* There were hidden dots deeply submerged beneath those stories that connected.

I heard the dialogues from a priest who would come each day after my father had passed away and shared the Shiva-Parvati dialogues in daily tranches building layer by layer. This went on for 9 days and each evening we would sit, he would converse in the Kashmiri language, and we heard his sharing.

In the first few days, I thought that the priests had evolved all this to point out to the people left behind, living and grieving, perspectives on not sinning and therefore if they do that, not to be afraid of death. Maybe also to offer hope of an after world so that we felt that the departed had just transitioned and was not *dead and gone*, it was just the physical shell that had died.

I marvelled at the fact that someone aeons ago had realised that the people present and at such time, hearing the discourses, were malleable and had an influenceable state of mind, so was an ideal opportunity to bend them in, what the priests perceived to be the *right* thinking and the correct directions. That the stories shared were nudges to people to live life the right, righteous and moral way. All this to a captive, receptive and engaged audience!

There obviously was the essence of a sermon being delivered. In many instances, a multitude of explanation of rituals got added, as also shlokas (verses) from the Indian holy texts -the Vedas, the Bhagwat Gita and Ramayana. The storyline was built around the journey of a soul after death. All the addons led the needle, the secret, getting lost in the haystack.

Months later, one day when I was remembering and reflecting upon all that had been said that I had the eureka moment. As the dots connected, the fog lifted, and the underlying theme emerged. As I dwelled upon this intriguing theme, I could segregate the stories, the dialogues, strip away the admonishments, the interwoven fables and began to see clearly, the thought-provoking theme within it all with stark clarity. The dots connected into something immensely powerful!

With some excitement I drew and wrote out the seven governing principles onto paper in concentric circles, I was amazed at what I had discovered. Perhaps, rediscovered the secret would be the right word!

Then as I thought of and delved deeper into each element, it started making even greater sense – the arrangement, the framework, was awesome. I started exploring these elements further with w*hat-if-this* and *what-if-that* and I found to my surprise that the model held up firmly and the model was in fact quite practical, even dynamic in operation yet very capable of being adjusted to circumstance.

Here I must mention another important context. Dharma and actions are completely interlinked, as only when the actions are done or not done that the doing or not doing of Dharma happens. It is by action choices only that the deed is done.

Clearly, before any actions are done, there are thoughts that exist that lead to action and even beneath the thoughts, there are feelings and intentions as well as inner constructs individual to each person. We will explore the linkages more deeply in the later chapters. However, first, let us examine the realm of actions.

The context to Karma

In the *7CircleDharma* I will use the word Karma as related to your action or inaction and, also in an added sense, related to consequences. The Dharma part concerns the correctness of action. The Karma sense used here is the action and its consequences.

We need to be clear about what Karma is, in the *7CircleDharma* sense, and importantly, what it is not. For example, our usage is values based and not religion or spirituality based.

Karma means action, work, or deed. As per Wikipedia it also refers to the spiritual principle of cause and effect where the intent and actions of an individual influence the future of the individual. Some extend the cause-effect across rebirth scenarios and this is not the context in using the word Karma in the *7CircleDharma.*

In this book, the connection of this life's actions to the next life is not the exploration. It is the connection between Dharma and the action-intent aspects. Here and now is all that matters. This interweaving reality between Dharma and Karm exists. It will be useful to connect karma also in the sense of being a Karam Yogi – one who performs the right actions.

Let us also understand some other contexts in which Karma is talked of.

Karma has been talked about by many, from the God Vishnu's incarnation as Krishna's directions and alternatively on to

Buddhist renderings, yet onwards to thousands of interpretations by scholars and experts each one adding their own bit. You want to read more details on Karma, with a spiritual/religious connect then read one of those other books and you will find many.

I need to talk about it, Karma, in its core simplicity. Also, as I said earlier, it has a direct connection in the contexts of Dharma.

Karma in another sense is concerned with the aftereffect of each action you perform. Each action also obviously has an internal connect within you, the why you did what you did; emotional or mental. Those of a religious frame of mind would call it a spiritual connect. Our connect is arising at the point of values you live by and their rendering inside you and onwards to the repercussions of the actions you perform.

Some actions are merely task-related and are the work part of the action. It is the minute that the action took birth in your mind, that the intent behind drove it to happen, that is the essence that relates to Karma in the 7 Circles. The intent behind is also the key connect to Dharma, in fact, is the common ground in a way.

Karma is different from plain simple physical action in the sense that was it a *right* action or otherwise. And in either case, right or wrong, the repercussions follow.

The clear connection of some past action (or even inaction) in your life resulting in a current situation, happens to be easily provable and in fact may have been the birth point of Karmic theory.

The easiest theme extension would obviously be to attach a future happening to a current action which is fine. (This then also started extending, even to the extent of a current reality looping back into a past life action and current action on to impacting the next life situations.) So, beyond what logic cannot explain, religion can!

Compounded to this was that we humans grew up programming our mind based on knowledge, tools, methods, languages and more such influences as existed at that time in their immediate environment. As the mind expands so do the questions.

Ultimately grew up learning language, social skills, other skills to become a self-contained unit afloat on this earth. At which time (s)he invariably asked, who am I, what am I, what purpose do I serve, why was I born and why will I die… the individual's ego, not in a negative sense, takes over the questioning.

The promise of an after life of grander constructs were tools religions used either to set up fears or rewards and thus mankind progressed corralled into inherited cultural beliefs, societal or religious or even family, tribe or nation.

When religions were invented and thereafter practised, they arose and flowed in many directions as humankind was prone to face worries, anxieties, fears, uncertainty, threats, disruptions, death, and misery. Then there is the fact that there were good times apart from the bad times or even good and bad feelings people had encountered.

Drawing a plausible and accepted story on how and why this good and bad occurs possibly begat religions. In a way, each religion is a set of stories and related edicts that we subscribe to and hold to be true.

So, the usual admonition was, Karma the fate that awaits due to past actions, even as many claim arising from our past lives with the reality and situation they faced now, this embedded belief in them on rebirth and Karma.

Then there is the other facet of Karma, being a Karm yogi, doing the actions right as the need to act arises. This is more in consonance with the *7CircleDharma* approach.

Getting away from more detail, possible debates and complexities I get back to my renderings.

Each action we take has repercussions. Some consequences are good some bad, some neutral.

It is not just Karma of the past life if you so believe. The Dharma is done or not done in this life, in this very moment where we decide to do and act. So more relevant from the perspective of this *7CircleDharma* is the present life and the now instant.

For example, if you did not study well in the earlier years of your life, then this Karma catches up in later life into your possibilities or lack of them. Karma has momentum!

So, Karma is the action and repercussions of the actions. Dharma is the why and how to decide what to do (or not to do) so that we can end up doing what is right.

In India, if we did the right thing, they said you have done your Dharma. If wrong, then they said Adharma (without dharma).

Yardsticks will greatly vary for each one of us based on our locations, religions and education or other influences. These yardsticks and the *7CircleDharma* will determine whether you have done the *right* action or the *wrong* one. For repercussions usually follow, they say, in the Karmic sense.

Ethics and morality are similar in a sense except that in moral behaviour the definition of right and wrong is based on whatever god and religion you subscribe to and are guided by.

Ethical is based on a set of principles, based on positive values that you take ownership of and the resultant do's and don'ts.

Legal on the other hand will be based on the laws in your realm that prescribe what is permissible and what is not as also the penalty of breaking laws.

What defines right, what defines wrong… therein lies the

debate and often the dilemmas! The *7CircleDharma* will demystify this greatly.

What is clear is that your thinking precedes all actions or inactions. It follows that action or Karma, or its consequences are a separate domain and what goes on in the mind defining and creating or setting up actions is another thing, these, the setting up of actions in the mind, are the aspects that concern Dharma.

Back to Dharma

Now coming to the dictionary definitions of Dharma as these would give some context to what it is traditionally understood as.

Merriam-Webster:

a. the basic principles of cosmic or individual existence: divine law
b. conformity to one's duty and nature.

The *Oxford* dictionary (on Lexico):

a. the eternal and inherent nature of reality, regarded in Hinduism as a cosmic law underlying right behaviour and social order.
b. the nature of reality regarded as a universal truth taught by the Buddha.
c. An aspect of truth or reality.

And *Collins*:
social custom regarded as a **religious** and **moral** duty.

Thus, the words, social, moral, reality, conformity, principles, nature, behaviour, social order, custom and duty draw the broad essence of what Dharma is. Added to this are legal aspects that govern. From the perspective of this *7CircleDharma,* the added-on word is ethical based on principles that we will share with you.

Perhaps at the back of it all, there are strands of values you hold dear, positives ones that influence and are in turn influenced by where you are and what inherited beliefs surround you. Lurking also are the negative ones and these also can take root.

This coalesces over a period of time as you grow up and a few dominant values take root in your mind. In normal existence, these mostly stay undisturbed, though some addons do occur.

Deep within us are values we hold dear or values that we have adopted. The positive ones generate a positive outlook, and the negative ones generate the opposite. They decide which side of the fence you reside. It is not just enough to claim values, you must live by them!

These then weave into habit patterns and you have automated negative or positive thoughts that arise and run your life. The thinking machine behind it gets often switched off. Yet the mind is aware and sooner or later catches up sometimes too late. Our exploration is to give our attitudes – the ways we think a solid foundation, that of *7CircleDharma.*

How we think and behave

It is interesting to note that our behaviour is in a large way influenced by 5 broad factors. Beliefs, convictions, herd behaviour, influencers, and habits.

Beliefs are inherited thoughts we carry of what people and generations held to be true or false, wrong or right, done or not done and thou shalt and thou shall nots. These are based on what people before us discovered, adopted and held true. These have been passed on to us starting from a noticeably young age.

These beliefs can be societal, religious, political, cultish, familial, things that previous generations held/hold to be true and passed on to us to form a significant part of our mindset.

Then are the convictions. These are based on our experiences, things we, on our own, came to conclusions about, in the passage of our lives and got recorded in us to add another dominant layer to our mindset. These are the I cant's, the I can's, the I do, the I don'ts types of messages your nebulous mind puts forth.

Some aspects may also reside in limbo as we fail to reach firm conclusions on many things we encounter as they are in some kind of unresolved state. These tend to paralyse our actions and more often than not we become susceptible to what others tell us. Lack of convictions or a very low level also has impacts as the person is for ever seeking other people's opinions and not in control of his or her life.

The convictions band can exist in form of learnings to be drawn upon intuitively. Or conclusions we drew and also the debilitating state of confusion and waywardness. There thus may be many anxieties and fears that run parallel to each state and at times are responsible for our many inconsistencies.

The third is herd behaviour. No matter what you hold true or false, what you think are your principles by which you live life by, there are times when group thinking hijacks you and your own belief, convictions are left on the wayside. You start doing things everyone is doing. The duration of this herd mindset can be short or sometimes long. Yet it controls your behaviour in a way as if your mind has shut off.

The herd mindset can be seen in a variety of situations,

fashion, trending things, sports, wars, politics, riots and even compassionate help to give you some examples. Some emotional connect always forms the base glue of this herd thinking. Group behaviour influences are present much more than we consciously realise. Here a collective kind of mind starts operating and our own mind takes backstage.

I mentioned habits, these primarily arise out of conditioning, repeatedly doing the same thing many times over. We thus settle into patterns of existence. These are shortcuts the mind creates and are related to the other 4 aspects. Why these are important is because you need to correct or improve a pattern, a series of repeated actions of the same kind, then you need to work on changing the habit, else a poorer one will always let you down. These can condition you to win or fail.

Embedded habits can gain you consistency in Adharma or Dharma depending on the habit.

Finally, are the tribe, the influencers. These could be people who gain a national image, they inspire, you respect their words with an implicit trust that they evoke. They could be events that shape destinies. Events like what we are witnessing for George Floyd. Then personalities that emerge as beacons, people like Gandhi or Marx who moved people into intuitive relatable directions. There can also be people like Hitler; people who can move the masses, sway us into directions they choose and ones that may not have been our intuitive or logical choices, and with hindsight appear to have been poor directions. Influencers fundamentally brainwash you in one way or the other.

These influencers have an amazing capability of saying things that capture your imagination, and in actual reality, it also captures your mind. Somewhere, something resonates clearly or inexplicably; endears, outrages – always has some emotional connect, paves a pathway to your feelings. Thus, the logical part of your brain only ends up playing a role in justifying your alignment. At other times polarising you with opposite feelings. The influencer often ends us subduing its opposing feeling by repeat messaging. True or false does not matter as a relentless barrage of repeat messaging moulds your mental landscape.

The Nazi, Joseph Goebbels defined the law of propaganda, 'Repeat a lie often enough and it becomes the truth'.

This outrageously sad thing is being used even today by people to meet their own objectives. The sad thing is they are based on a bundle of lies which can directly be traced back to some bad intent or negative desires.

Rumours are a mass instance of faceless influencers at work, your mind stripped of separating truth from untruth, gets influenced… though the rumours are different in the sense that they do not have sustained impact. The posts on social media can be a special class of rumours that leverage the digital and play on gullibility. Somehow people irrationally are compelled with the thought – I have read it so this must be true!

Thus, the influencers have emerged in another virtual avatar, which is the internet. Here your band of inherited beliefs and discovered convictions somehow take backstage. The ability to judge and accept information becomes a slave to the transaction at hand and you get up with what you think is a valid point of view. At times you use it to reinforce something or at other times it uses you to delude you. Of course, many times this is a useful source and that keeps you hooked on.

The point to note is that any of these external agendas, ones that influence your behaviour, can then be either leading you up the right path or they can be leading you to some wilderness or moral and emotional ruin. You have, of course, the freedom of choice - and only if you recognise it and consciously exercise it! The danger being overwhelmed by the influencers!

Of these famous four, only the convictions arise within your span of control and from your experiences. The rest are external influences. You are not living life the way you want to; you are living life the way they want you to live. We have fed our mind with these external software patches and programmed ourselves to a situation that we stray in many different directions, not all of them good.

The fifth, habits, are conditioned and adopted patterns so internal.

Back to what I had discovered

Coming back to what I shared at the start of this chapter. The stories the priest told us and my discovering a hidden treasure within it.

Sometimes I think that what I share here must be the foundations from where those elaborate stories and rituals started from as I heard the guru speak.

The core I discovered was the seven circles, and it seems that each generation of brahmins added to the narrative, embellished it with generous examples, built into it diverse moral and ethical lectures, wandered from the main points to designed it to fit quotes from other scriptures, perhaps to add authority. The core of the 7 circles framework kept getting lost in the fog of added words and the deluge of other references.

The narrative as I said, is a series of questions Parvati asks of Shiva and he replies in Kashmiri, *Hey Gatij, ch booz bu wanney.* (literally: *Oh, wise person, you hear, and I will tell you about it*) Then goes on to explain, this is from where I got the hints after stripping away many mundane questions and answers. Meantime the priest adds his appendages and the hugely important method on what to do and what not to do and how gets lost.

Let me retrieve the first core secret:

The start and the vital innermost circle, in your existence here on this planet, is YOU. If you cease to exist then the other circles do not matter, they evaporate into irrelevance. If you cease to empower yourself then you get hampered. We will get into detail on this in the next chapter on what YOU means in the context of the 7 Circles.

The logic and thought behind the 7 Circles of Dharma is to help you, in a non-religious and practical way to navigate and celebrate your life better as a good human. At peace with what you do and performing your Karma according to a set of principles that are sound and powerful and will unravel as we go further in this book.

Would you like to explore this?

CHAPTER 1

THE 7 CIRCLES

Our deeds determine us,
as much as we determine our deeds.
~ George Eliot

Before we go further, it is important to understand what the 7 Circles of Dharma are, as this is the key to everything in this book.

The seven circles define the priorities in play by which you will judge the situation on which you have to act and empower you to do the right things. The first circle has the first priority as it defines your very existence and then the subsequent circles are in lesser and lesser precedence.

Many variable contexts are at work and these we will explore as we go into each circle and beyond in the subsequent chapters.

There are various interplays amongst and within the circles and this at times shifts or shuffles the order of precedence. You will also discover how these dynamic movements pan out and work as we go along. Then are matters within our mind that have a huge bearing on our actions, these we will also look in detail as they can be the final determinants of what happens.

There are huge associated benefits as you move your life into a state of higher 'right' thinking and actions. Some of the benefits associated with ethical and value led behaviour are a lower level of stress, greater peace of mind and lower levels of conflict within as well as outside.

Additionally, when you are able to prioritise using the *7CircleDharma* your decision making becomes far easier and correct actions follow. This priortisation also helps you in ease of saying no to the things of lesser priority which helps you in turn to retain momentum and the flow of positive things in life.

The *7CircleDharma* will also help you lead a holistic and wholesome life and lesser guilt upon many things that bother you from time to time. Your emotional climate improves leading to greater satisfaction in the things you do.

It will also quickly produce clarity in situations you face resulting in timely action and a sharper focus on things that ought to be done. You will do more, cover more distance and achieve more in this journey of life. For many issues in life your problem-solving ability will improve as you will be able to discriminate between situations quite easily. You will find faster resolution in many conflicts.

You will also be able to look within you in a deeper sense and conquer glass ceilings or artificial limitations that you may have put on yourself. This will lead you to get to your potential and achieve more with a better and positive mindset.

There are huge benefits in the emotional band by adopting these practices as you will be able to take greater ownership of your desires, pursue things with better focus with an overall hugely positive emotional state of mind as you conquer the nagging thoughts and feelings that pull you down.

Ultimately the largest benefit is the peace of mind as this is something that all of us continually seek.

So now to the arrangements and structure of the 7 Circles. We will obviously go deeper into each circle to understand the What, How, When, Where, Which, Who etc. The core structure, however, makes it easy to understand and define what actions you perform and are they the right ones in your Dharma. This is a powerful and easy to use methodology that is very practical in many ways.

It may seem that complexity will increase as we add so many variables, not so, as the key on the next page will make it obvious that the construct is easy to understand and follow.

These are the 7 circles:

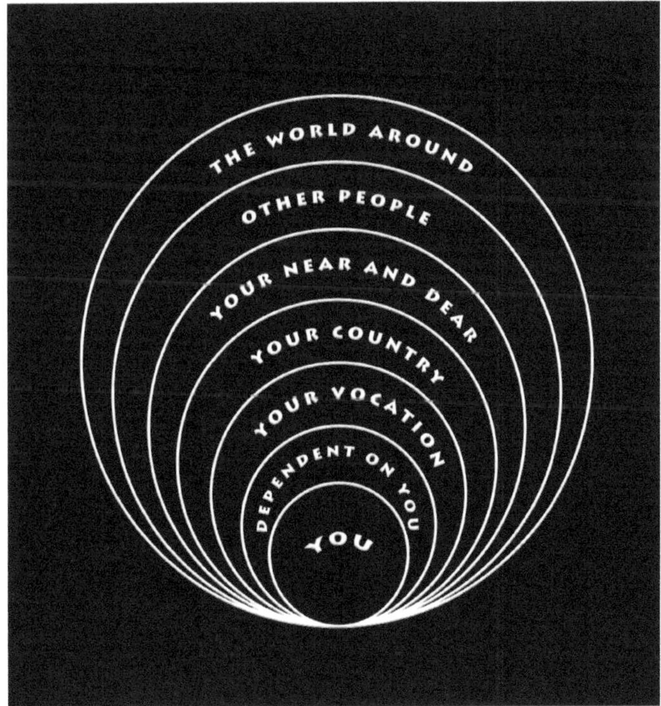

This is the Key

The First, innermost Circle, your first duty is to yourself. Not in a selfish way, but in a way that enhances you to do things with an outward-looking mindset, capable to perform at a peak level. You also need to pair this with an aware, agile and responsive mindset towards the external environment. It is the solid base that empowers you to do your duty to yourself and others. The key theme is: empower yourself.

The Second Circle, the next concentric circle, is your duty to those who are dependent on you in one way or another. The key theme is: take personal responsibility.

The Third Circle is your duty to what we call your *annadata*, which means your vocation. This could mean the company you work for, the business you run, the avenues that provide you with financial sustenance. The key theme is: be true to your calling.

The Fourth Circle is the duty to your country, in the sense to the place where you live in some kind of mental and physical security. The key theme is: do your duty to keep yourself and others secure.

The Fifth Circle is your duty to people who you are related to, your friends as also other people you have met or who you know. The key theme is: we are social beings.

The Sixth Circle, the duty to other humans even though you do not know them or have even not met them. Humankind. The key theme is: look beyond yourself.

The Seventh Circle is your duty towards the environment and nature that surrounds us. The key theme is: justice to planet earth.

Dharma is always practiced in two areas; one is Dharma towards yourself and the other is Dharma towards others. It is critical to remember that YOU by itself, solo and purely self-gain centred in intent and based on a predominant selfish purpose is a sure recipe for disaster and Adharma.

Unless the YOU is paired with others outside you and responsive to their entitled benefits, it will not function to the complete set of Dharma actions.

When you think of YOU, it is also to enable you to honestly feed the outer circle responsibilities and do that with an attitude of fairness.

This is the defining framework of the 7 circles of Dharma. When you use these *7CircleDharma* principles you get free of stress and guilt, you solve dilemmas, you do not waste time in endless mental debates, you feel good at what you do are doing and you know you have done the right thing!

Unless you confront internal barriers and throw off the stories you tell yourself you will not open your mind to listen and discover. Go with an open mind!

You can make your life simple and uplifting by being mindful of the *7CirclesDharma* or remain exhaustingly complex if you do not. The choice is yours!

Want to know how to do this, read on…

CHAPTER 2

THE FIRST CIRCLE
I AM TILL I REMAIN

Intent defines what you think and try.

I am not here to challenge the rebirth of the soul theories. Let us for the present take care of this birth and our existence on this planet. As we exist now, today, this very moment.

The *7CirclesDharma* is all about this moment. As you think so do you act. Your behaviour is just a reflection of your actions. It is about doing the right actions. The action of *now*. The next moment is the next act. So, focus on the now. On your response to what is happening around you, now. These actions you perform, at times even not perform, directly and irrevocably reflect you doing or not doing Dharma. When the right action is not done then it is called Adharma.

One has to exist to be able to respond. And the word 'exist' just does not mean just to be alive. It means your state of existence as an entity, the complete you. Mentally fit, physically fit, emotionally balanced, capable of meeting your needs, capable of doing what all you need to do with lessening constraints. Also, all this being done with a host of logical elements and emotional elements mixed in as you respond to volatile external circumstance and emerging conditions.

Willing, enabled and capable to act right.

So, do whatever you need to do to be able to perform your Dharma to its fullest potential.

The first circle, the innermost, the first Dharma, as we mentioned, you fulfil is towards YOU. Again, the caution, not in a selfish egoistic mindset, but rather in a type of an evolving existence that also thinks beyond oneself.

A caution here. YOU is not stated as a feed to your selfish ego. The purpose behind, the intent you have, is the key. Is your purpose only self-gain, then it is not the right purpose in our context.

The key purpose of addressing yourself in the first circle is to empower yourself to do for others when the need demands it besides the need to prosper, grow and evolve to your best possibilities.

It means you exist well in a balanced way and are capable of existing for extended periods of time empowered to respond and operate with a positive mind that overcomes circumstance. It also means that you drive yourself to your own peak potential.

Let me summarise the seven circles again:

- Your first duty is towards you existing and performing well to be able to do all the rest.
- Your second duty is towards people dependent on you.
- Your third duty is towards anything that provides you sustenance, your business, your profession, the company you work for – anything vocation connected.

- Your fourth duty is towards your country, or the area you live in that provides you with a secure habitat.
- Your fifth duty is to people you know, relatives, friends, acquaintances.
- Your sixth duty is towards the rest of the people in the world.
- Your seventh duty is to the world around you, the planet Earth!

We will get into the interplays the whys, the what's the how's, the when and the where and which as we go from chapter to chapter. We will also go into how your mind works while handling all this.

The circle's borders are nebulous, an example:

Suppose you are on the road and someone has an accident. You do not know the person. People you do not know are in the sixth circle. However as soon as this person is injured, requires help, perhaps needs to be taken to the hospital, he or she is a person dependent on you then at that point in time. (S)he has, maybe even for a few hours, moved into your second circle, and thus your dharma is to come to his/her aid.

More of this later, let us get back to YOU.

YOU have several dimensions, facets-aspects that you must consider and even more besides these will be relevant.

Physical	Mental	Capability
Security	Survival	Recognition
Prosperity	Motivation	Positivity
Values	Social	Resources
Trust	Interests	etc.

There may be many other aspects, all connected and related to what strands make you up as a unique individual. Your unique personal situation will define what other elements you need to look into.

For example, you may have special talents, say an inherent gift for music and sing well. You may be a good sportsperson. So, there may be strengths, unique talents, you have, interests you have or could add on. There could be an astounding natural talent in you for something. Even thinking about what you could be good at starts a process of discovery. To build on something existing or to acquire something new. This question will add customised dimensions to your interests, desires and priorities.

The whole idea is that YOU have to be in a mode where you can perform what you need to perform as also, importantly, to excel in. Any weak link here reduces your capability to respond when you are faced with a choice of action. Any undeveloped areas will cheat you of opportunity.

Whatever level you are at you have to constantly strive to be better than yesterday, this leads you to move purposefully to your overall potential and possibilities. This is the source attitude and quest that helps people grow and mature.

This enhancing yourself, perhaps in multiple dimensions, has to be the mainstay of your journey in the 1st Circle and as you add strength to each dimension, you create awesome freedom for yourself to exercise your Dharma and act with good Karma.

But what if you are weak in any of these aspects at a given point in time? Does that mean you cannot, should not, will not act with Dharma? Absurd to think so. You have to think right and act right, the best you can, despite circumstance, situations and capability.

In the example I shared, a bystander to that accident, could very well call upon others to help, call the ambulance, call the police, within his/her constraints doing his/her Dharma. Walking away is Adharma.

So, the intention to do, to act is a cornerstone of Dharma. The rest are constraints and obstacles, and yet if you do genuinely what you can, you have done your Dharma.

Doing nothing, particularly when you could have done something and not getting blocked off by obstacles and not seeking solutions then clearly means that you may have not done your Dharma. For Dharma is irrevocable done only when you act in a positive direction.

Having said that, there will be times when you ponder, you may have conflicting choices, be on the horns of a dilemma. Sure, think you must but not for so long that the moment of action, of karma, passes. Then your inaction becomes your Karma. There is always an impacting difference between pausing and stopping!

What to do when faced with options? The easiest way out is to think of the *7CirclesDharma* as this will help you say yes or no to whatever the corresponding option is. The seven circles are your priorities yardstick!

Let us know start by looking at ways you can do Dharma to yourself.

Your Physical self

Your physical fitness is important if this declines then you reduce your capability. When the time comes your performance can and will surely be impaired.

So, the first question is, in this aspect of maintaining and sustaining your physical wellbeing towards peak levels. These aspects empower you. So where-am-I in health and fitness levels are the first dimensions you should examine. The old adage says health is wealth and not without a reason.

Are you doing your Dharma to yourself with regard to your Physical self? Are you doing, not doing, doing enough, doing the best, not ignoring, building, sustaining? The level, the progress or the standstill!

If there is a gap in these, discover what your first actions will be because your journey within the first circle has just started. When you start asking the right questions: Where am I and where I ought to be, then this gap leads you to the Dharma actions you can do.

Your Mental self

Second, is your mental well being and upliftment. Again questions are the right source to identify what you must do. Like: What are you doing to have your mind in top gear? Do you have a positive mindset? Are you continuously learning? What kind of things do you need that will enhance your success in terms of your career or vocation? If you have stress in your mind, what is the cause? And what can you do to minimise the impact of the stressor? Do you generally think positive or have a large number of negative thoughts? Do you overcome fears, anxieties and worries?

The best is not to play mental juggling when you think of such aspects. Write whichever ones are important to you, put them down on paper and then think through them. Sleepover what you have thought through and the next day, relentlessly look for solutions, actions to do. This too is your Dharma!

These are not just one time exercises you must do. Life is a journey, and you must set periodic milestones to revisit, reflect and discover more enhancements and then act upon a plan to enhance. You must cultivate an open mind only then you can grow.

A second aspect concerns what we feed our minds. Is it principally garbage or is it something worthwhile? With the advent of social media there is a free flow of information, texts, clips, stories and many of these can be poor messaging into your mind. At times it may be an inconsequential and useless burden on your mind. Discipline is needed from your end to exert some control and maintaining such discipline is your Dharma.

A vitally important part of you is your mindset and it is your Dharma to keep enhancing this.

Your Behaviours

We all settle into habits, good or bad. Some people get angry, some are meek. Some people are responsive, some reticent. Some people procrastinate, others are always jumping the gun. Some talk too much some talk too little. Some listen well and some do not allow others to talk. Some are focused and others distracted. Some well organised some always lost.

Sometimes we have blind spots so it is useful to ask others to give their suggestions on where they think you should change. Listen to learn and not to debate. Do fully avoid getting defensive, overly argumentative or reactive.

What are your pain points? Some you may discover on your own and some from others. Add them to your dharma list!

Fixing behaviours that let you down is your Dharma. Enhancing positive behaviour is also your Dharma.

Your Capability Matrix

We always need competencies in several areas, know what to do and know how to do – makes you competent. However, *Capability* comes out of a bundle of competencies working together.

An example would be in order. Supposing you have good competencies in accounting and finance. You may have good analytical skills, but you lack some key competence in using computers for the work you are doing. Thus, despite having a few key competencies, the absence of ones required to complete the bundle lowers your capability and your performance.

There are a core band of competencies, these are a must-have kind, and any gaps here will make you disempowered. Beyond these are, of course, competencies related to your trade, vocation, hobby or key interests you pursue.

There are a host of competencies that can exist. Some are core, like staying organised, managing your time, managing goals, communication, practiced empathy and skills needed for working with others. Do ensure you have the core band covered.

If you are more capable you can always do more for yourself and others. What do you need to do to move up a notch in one or more of the competencies? What is holding you back? What is stopping you from your potential? This should be an unending quest. It has been said that questions are answers, if you do not ask the question, you will never know the answer.

To keep building your mindset, competencies, effectiveness and capability to higher levels is your Dharma.

Your security aspects

These can in turn have different dimensions, not just physical security. For example, it can include, family security, income security, the security of your own home, security of your career or future. The absence of any one of these types, even low levels of these, will instil anxiety and fear. Introspection is how you will discover where you are in such aspects. Gnawing worries often divert you from clear thinking. Fix this!

Do you need to build further in these? Which ones are the weakest links? Where are the gaps? Introspect often and regularly.

You need to not only discover these but do something to address them, this is your Dharma.

The survival imperative

Maslow was a social scientist and developed the hierarchy of needs. He put survival at the core and base of all human needs.

Most people may be past this survival band in normal times and be more concerned with the next band of security- for example of a job, access to good education etc. Yet there are times we can face threats to our survival and security with small or large threats lurking.

The current Covid crisis has bought this to the fore globally and without exception. The prime need is survival. Remember the first circle is YOU if you don't exist everything evaporates into irrelevance.

Faced with situations where your survival is threatened, your Dharma is to do what it takes to survive. This may also extend to the survival of others in a sense.

It of course includes shunning any reckless, impulsive or other irresponsible behaviours. All this needs to be done with positive actions and a positive frame of mind.

Clearly in today's context, with the Covid crisis; wearing a mask, avoiding large gatherings and keeping social distancing is your Dharma.

And if you do not do what you need to do you are doing Adharma to yourself and others.

The prosperity imperative

They say money is not everything, may appear to be quite true when you look at it in a philosophical sense. Yet money, in reality, does extend your capability to do things. It empowers you to do things for yourself and also empowers your Dharma to give and do for others, the absence of money may restrict you most times. You may be agonisingly willing but painfully unable.

In most cases the challenge is not YOU pursuing prosperity, the challenge can often be that you get so busy in doing that pursuit and miss out on doing other things that you ought to have done for other circles and other areas of life beyond making money. The Dharmic quest is always a proper balance.

If you look at people like Bill Gates, who perhaps will qualify to be described to be at the pinnacles of prosperity, we find that beyond a level he starts giving back to society and feeding the prosperity into avenues of the other circles. We can live in our cocoon or try and discover a whole new world outside.

So, give back, as your prosperity increases, so do enhance your capability to look beyond your self and reach out and contribute purposefully to the outer circles. That too is your Dharma.

Increasing your prosperity levels is also one of your fundamental Dharma. This in turn will empower you and facilitate your fantastic support to other circles. Each one of us has potential to do many things for ourselves and others yet failing to see the potential is a barrier.

Motivation breaks inertia

Ultimately it is your desires within, linked to purposeful goals that generate motivation. These invariably fuel the progress, movement and momentum of your life.

Lack of motivation drives a person into an inward prison of inaction and leads to a waste of potential. Lack of it will also generate prime barriers of I cant's within you, preventing you from helping yourself and helping others. Lack of it will also promote procrastination and avoidance of responsibility.

Not learning how you can stay motivated, even in the face of adversity, is something each one has to develop. Not knowing how and doing nothing to change this is the extreme Adharma you can do to yourself. The secret is simple and is to revisit your inner dreams and desires often.

Lack of motivation also traps you into comfort zones and plateaus of existence as opportunity keeps passing you by. Motivated people on the other hand become proactive and find ways to overcome and succeed. They constantly reach out and open doors.

Self-motivation is a learnable thing. As one surfaces out accomplishments or revisits things that one should be grateful for builds a positive sense inside us and start building within us a belief that we can do more.

To understand this, spare a moment even right now and reflect on a few things, maybe one, two three things that you are most grateful for in your life. If you extend this by writing these down and then writing why you are grateful you will see the magic happen and the sense of motivation touching you. Try it!

A simple habit of daily reflection on at least one thing that made you happy that day will boost you a few notches higher. Writing a daily journal of accomplishments makes it more powerful as you can always flip through and revisit to recharge your batteries! Even small victories count and add the layers. Once you are in a motivated state it becomes contagious as you charge up not only yourself but also others.

Motivating yourself, staying motivated and motivating others is your Dharma.

Positivity

Hope has been the eternal spring that sustains all mankind. The vision of a better future relative to where you are, the desire to move to that future state and the willingness to do what it takes. All these cannot be done without positive mindsets.

An element of self-belief is also vitally necessary. The absence of dreams, hope or belief automatically produces negative thoughts. And when these appear, so do their relatives – anger, frustration and negative emotions. These tragically drown you into deeper abysses of negativity.

The core of positivity is a mindset that is constantly seeking solutions. So, one needs to be solution-centric rather than problem-centric. We talk of positive thinking, which is not just affirmations but also includes a solution thinking mindset.

Maintaining that positive outlook in life is your Dharma.

Values

Ultimately it is the WHY behind your WHAT you do that matters most. These why's from your inner self will always have connections to the values you hold dear. They will also be where your 'intent' resides. At times, the why's may slide towards the opposing negatives that you may have cultivated, shun those. On the other hand, positive values are the ones that propel you to your Dharma and help you stay directed.

So, what are these values? There are many and some interrelated. Here we are talking of positive values.

A sample list below shows you some that have positivity and can represent a state of mind and helps you discover actions you can take related to that element.

Courage	Gratitude	Non-Violence
Equality	Happiness	Optimism
Fairness	Honesty	Peace
Faith	Humility	Respect
Family	Joy	Selflessness
Fun	Justice	Service delight
Generosity	Loyalty	Sincerity
Goodness	Love	Truth
Care	Integrity	Tolerance
Reliability	Adventure	Friendship
Freedom	Justice	Fulfilment

You can add to the list. An important source could be from the religion you profess. Christian, Muslim, Hindu or other does not matter. Each religion has several positive values deeply embedded in its core and in its preaching. Add from there, it will also help you discover ones that may be most important to you. You may also discover ones relevant to you from the ideologies and/or philosophies you subscribe to. One may resonate with many of these, but the quest is to discover and identify the top ones that hold greater meaning to you.

To find the top ones, for example, you can circle the top 10 in the overall list you make, ones that you relate to strongly. Do not overanalyse and do it quickly so that it comes from your subconscious. Then select the top 5 that your heart cannot delete.

Reflect on the top 5 each day identify actions you did or could have done that align your actions to values. This will help you program your mind so that APT starts. (Automated Positive Thoughts) This programs your mind into a Dharma capable positive mindset.

The qualifying question is, which ones do you hold dear, which ones come spontaneously to you in an intuitive way, the ones that your heart cannot delete. A good pathway to self-enhancement is to work consciously on each one for a month or so that your mindfulness on it increases. A good idea is to work one by one and we can always repeat the focus attention on any further ones that you wish to grow next as and when needed.

You will note that many of these are not self-centred. They come into play when you do unto others.

It is not enough for you to say, these are my principal values, do you exemplify them by your actions? When you do, you truly become authentic.

To consistently reflect them authentically in your actions is your Dharma.

One more aspect is important. What are you led by when you act in favour of YOU? Is it anger, revenge, greed or some other negative aspect? Then this is not the YOU of Dharma. Such people get held in a vice that ultimately chips away and destroys the YOU and builds and sustains Adharma.

What this means is that it is not enough to say I have positive values, you must cleanse yourself inside of you of any negatives, then only you will empower yourself for Dharma. The only way of cleansing out is to displace them with positiveness the increased practice of which will crowd out the negatives. Of course, you can identify the negatives and say a firm no to yourself whenever the thoughts arise.

Many times, we reinforce behaviours that oppose the positive values that we seek to adopt.

There was a person who used to get angry very often. Even though, after the outburst, he would feel remorse and think he should not have lost his cool, invariably he would come up with some rationalisation. 'I always get angry whenever someone does anything stupid'. This sentence is the mini-story he would keep telling himself.

He would keep repeating this sentence, true as it may have been, so many times that he did not realise that this very thing kept locking him further and further into undesirable behaviour. He had set up a programmed negative thought pattern in his mind.

Unless he stops saying that and replaces it with a positive affirmation on staying cool, nothing will change.

Do you have these mini-stories you tell yourself that stop you from adopting positive values in your life?

Let me give you some examples of what mini-stories we can be telling ourselves and without realising that as you think in such a manner it invariably propagates the negative thought and behaviours - onwards every time you repeat them.

- I always get angry when…
- I always forget to…
- I am always failing to…
- I feel confused…
- I always overreact...

These are some examples of mini-stories you tell yourself, all can be some Programmed Negative Thoughts that consume the YOU inside you.

Getting rid of them is your Dharma.

Self-knowledge, keeping track of ME, *where-am-I* and *where-I-need-to-change* is a vital responsibility that one should have. Investing time for such self-development is top Dharma.

Social aspects

No one exists well in isolation. We have evolved as a species into becoming social beings, interacting and interdependent.

Do you live in a cocoon? Is the only person you do something for always you?

The outward outlook you possess has a great bearing on your Dharma, as an absence of this outward reach cuts you off from the other circles. Unless you reach out you will be limiting your own possibilities, living an incomplete life.

Look beyond yourself is, therefore, your Dharma.

Reputation and Trust

What one thinks of oneself can at times be quite different from what others think about us. We do have many blind spots. At times we may have some failing and yet we tend to invent some justification and keep cultivating that failing. All such impact your reputation.

In your pursuit of things in life, many things come into play. Principally it is the behaviour patterns that project out to others what they perceive you to be. This defines your personality as it appears to others.

Your behaviour in the context of honestly, dependability and sociability will have a huge bearing on whether people trust you or not and what reputation you form.

Just having the right intent is not enough, you should be seen exemplifying such.

Besides the personality, it is your character that is vitally important. The character connects to positive values, a sense of judgement and compassion. These when reflected in your actions also feed what other people think of you.

Trust is the magic magnet that creates success.

It comes about only if you care about others and do things that demonstrate your care. It is aided by a feeling of genuine concern about the other in their well-being and progress.

Trust can be built in an instant if you touch the others deep need to the core and help them find avenues or solutions that move them towards need fulfilment.

There is one more aspect of trust, how much you trust others, this we have to do all the time. However, be cautious of blind trust and if you get inklings that things are not moving in the right directions then respond immediately.

These are hugely important aspects that have a direct bearing on your personal and professional success in life.

It would be obvious that the 'I am' has far more aspects than the mere physical aspects. Your personality, your character, your interests, your natural capabilities, your strengths, your ability to manage interpersonal relationships, your constantly striving to evolve – in fact your vision in several dimensions all are relevant. Yet we seldom spend time on dwelling on ourselves and figuring out what we come across to others!

So, the composite of what you are, what you can become has direct connections to your values, your purposes, your nature (disposition) and the habits (mindset) that you have formed. This composite is also in constant flux depending on your emotional state – your feelings.

This feelings-emotion binds us, and many times becomes a principal barrier within us. This is the prime battle arena of Dharma, to rise above the feelings, seek out the why behind the what. This emotion led force sets up the conflict and can freeze us into inaction or veer us into wrong directions and corral us into wrong actions. However, if the feelings relate to the positive programmed thoughts these lead you to Dharma and so the feelings-emotions can also raise a person to great heights.

Emotion is something that cannot weigh in the consequences. It outplays logic. The key is to keep positive emotions into play and not let negative emotions impair your actions. The pause is a must for the emotion to settle down and only then you act.

Acting while keeping your emotion under control is your Dharma.

There are a plethora of other forces acting as barriers to Dharma. Greed, lust, anger, egoistic callings, an inability to refuse, lack of discipline, fear, revenge, cruelty, resigned-defeated attitude, fears and suchlike further fuel the emotion-logic confusion of the mind.

Perhaps you have to stay with the issue long enough for the emotional states to die down and subside, only then can you uncover the truth – the logical truth, the truth of dharma and face that as the prime issue.

The emotional disposition tainted with untruths can only be defeated when you see the truth without the emotional lenses.

As you proceed in your journey, you will discover many other aspects. One mention here of such is on how you manage your resources. How do you manage your money, wealth, possessions, your time spend, and finally how you manage your words… Mismanaging them is also Adharma.

Finally, this self-focus of the I-am-till-I-remain should not become a totally selfish pursuit.

The dedication to creating a capable and empowered self is different from self-centred obsessions.

There are battles of conflicting desires, obligations and many more things. We will explore these in the later chapters of this book as there is a high need to reconcile and handle these to stay on course.

When the key driver of our actions is holistic our actions will smoothly also flow to contribute to other people's well-being.

Dharma requires maintaining outward focus based on compassion and empathy.

So how would you score yourself, say on a scale of 1 to 10 in doing your Dharma?

Think about it.

PS: we are all work in progress.

CHAPTER 3

THE SECOND CIRCLE
A QUESTION OF POSITIVE DEPENDENCE

Desire binds others, love does not.

The second circle has people, things or endeavours that are dependant on you. If you do not do your Dharma, they suffer. They can be dependent on you in a variety of ways and situations. This dependence can be transactional or enduring.

Most of us, as we grow from our childhood years start forming the inner image of ourselves, this image at its core exists even inside our inner self in a corner of each one of us that is shared with no one else. This is a form of ego, the 'I' that has developed as we start growing up and striving to find a place and meaning in the adult world. This core is where we reside our desires, our yeas and nays. This is a core we seldom open out to others and beneath all this, the connected emotions and desires within us often rule our existence with finality.

Yet, one day, when this very adult has a child, this core melts and breaks down and absorbs the needs of the new-born as if it were the needs of the inner core. This then even merges a second circle into the first for the periods of the infancy of the child.

What happens is amazing and the merger, more so with mothers, sustains the tests of time, space and causation.

The duration of this merging varies from person to person. As the child grows and even if the merging stops, yet till he or she remains dependent on you will reside in your second circle.

The children you have, the wards you accept, the child you adopt they come into your second circle as you constantly strive, feel duty-bound, to meet their needs and help them navigate their life's journey to the best possible outcomes.

As it happens, one day this very person in your second circle will grow into adulthood, most times does get enabled to face the world on his/her own and not dependent on you for immediate needs, then they will migrate out for the physical aspects to an outer circle.

Not surprisingly, when that very parent becomes old and his/her first circle starts weakening in the capability of self-management, then the very child who had become an adult may find that the parent enters into his/her second circle.

The parent can be deeply or partially dependent emotionally, physically, economically or another way on the child who once was the second circle to that parent. The roles can reverse!

Now cultures may dictate, traditions may come into play, legal provisions may exist. Individual nature and character may impact. Those are circumstances.

The dependence of one person on another is not just financial, or a place to live. It extends beyond into hugely important emotional needs as well as the need to maintain their dignity.

The dependants may not just be your, spouse, (partner) or children. There are a host of others that may be in your second circle. As we go further these elements will surface out. Each one may have a varying degree of need and frequency of things they are dependant for.

The Dharma is clear, whoever is in a situation where they are directly dependent on you and you have directly or indirectly accepted them as such is in your second circle. You must do the right thing and your duty is to do that. It is your responsibility that you do not fall short in any way. That is your Dharma.

As we get into some key outer circles, we will cover sections on the circle concerning:

- Direct elements in the circle
- Transients - Visitors into the circle
- Frequently in and out
- Hierarchy
- Your Dharma in Times of conflict

The mentions in each such section are not in any priority related to the above sequence

DIRECT

Children: there are many aspects of what they depend on you for. From food, shelter, clothing, education, giving them the right values, having good times together, planning their development, protecting them from harm, growing them mentally, physically and emotionally. There are a huge number of facets you will be responsible for. Providing these is your Dharma.

Abandoning, not taking responsibility, blaming circumstance, venting frustration, any negative behaviour and suchlike are all Adharma.

Reflect back and discover where you stand, ask these types of questions to yourself:

- Should you be spending more time with your child?
- Do you have your communication lines open?
- Are you providing them with a 'good' example by your own behaviour?
- Are you working on their growth and future sufficiently?
- Are you patient with them?
- Do you encourage and motivate them?
- Are you there to help them when they encounter some difficulty?
- What kind of character do you project out?
- Do you motivate positively?
- Do you have fun times together?

Questions like these need to be asked. Again and again. Add any answers or gaps you discover you get to your Dharma list of actions.

The nature of your relationship with your child over each period of time has also to follow an evolving path. At a younger age, there may be more talking, telling, directing, explaining. Yet as the child grows the telling and ordering should be minimised and you have to get as near as possible to a facilitative approach based on honest sharing and asking questions, listening in place of directing and ordering.

It is your dharma is to evolve the relationship continuously and purposefully.

Possessions: Taking care of what you have, keeping them out of risk and danger also for possessions that are shared and sharable in the future is also your Dharma. This may apply to all kinds of assets.

While acquiring, managing and maintaining them may have been direct in your first circle, conserving them or utilising them to the best are second circle elements as they may also represent legacies to others.

The key driver here is when anything has the potential to be shared, it comes into the second circle as well. At many times this may be a form of trusteeship that you have to play out. Having said that each one of us is in a unique situation and having our own perspectives, which is fine.

Responsibilities you have accepted: This covers a wide swath! These may be to feed your family, to pay your bills, to deliver satisfaction to your 'customer', to do justice to roles you have taken on are some examples of what this facet of the second circle looks like.

It may be a small action like running an errand that you took on or can be a sustained number of actions. What you take on and say yes to enters your second circle.

Doing all the things that you need to do in all that you have taken on, by choice or chance, is your Dharma.

Promises you have given to others: Yes, in every sense this also can be called responsibility and can include small things as well as larger ones that you need to do. It can be one off things that are not necessarily as a continuum.

Be cautious then on what you say 'yes' to. This becomes a promise of a kind! It may have been better if you had said 'no'. Maybe a discovery in hindsight, but you have already made a promise. A further complication may arise when people assume your 'yes', so do pursue clarity.

Promises then, that get you in a situation where the other is, now, dependent on you fall squarely into your second circle.

To keep the promises made is your Dharma.

Having said that, if you find a reckless or casual yes landing you in a second circle responsibility it may be a good idea to go and convey regret and say no. Particularly in cases where this yes may mean devotion of your time, effort and resource that deny any 'direct' second circle element or a first circle imperative - then you go ahead and get yourself out of the situation, not by abandonment but by conveying your changed status of the promise.

In the Indian epics, one comes across several instances where a person is compelled to a line of action because he or she had given a *Vachaan.* (Vachaan = pledge or promise). At many times in the unfolding of the epic stories then lead the person to associate with or do acts of Adharma. This Vachaan as a justification to associate or continue to pursue, aid or abet Adharma is the highest wrong you can do.

Be wise, renegotiate, rescind it immediately if you see that the path of action is causing Adharma. Use the *7CircleDharma* and not the epic.

This does not mean that you do not keep your promises, only if you see that the promise is causing Adharma then only it is right to rework it. In normal situations all promises you have made should be kept!

There is no honour in doing something that causes harm to others.

Cheating your direct second circle elements of their due is Adharma. Cheating any higher circle of their due is Adharma.

Your Spouse or Partner: The needs may not just be physical or financial. Each one of us has great needs in the emotional bands.

Fulfilling all those needs is your Dharma.

It is said that good manners are just about respecting the dignity of others. This is true for all but particularly true for your partner. Yet we slip into criticism.

Frequent Criticism is a fine imposed on the mind
It reduces the other's self-esteem and self-belief

It is the reverse of recognition and progress
It outcasts the person

This brings forth the thought that wherever valid in the *7CircleDharma*, one has just not to look at the logic of the situation. Feelings matter and emotions are what make us human. Sensitivity, empathy are always prime needs. Using a mix of both logic and emotion complete you into a better person.

Striving always to maintain the dignity of your spouse and partner is your Dharma.

You will find that as you uphold the dignity of others, whether the expression includes physical or emotional elements, magic will happen.

Not having the sensitivity as a part of your being is Adharma.

Denying giving what you could easily have given, your love and respect, for example, is Adharma. Beyond these there could be others, brothers, sisters or relatives who depend on you.

People dependent on you for their livelihood: Yes, again may have the imprint of responsibility, and this is a mention of a class of others who are dependent on you.

Ones who directly are paid by you their wages of work or through an entity you own, or control would fall into this bracket.

Giving such people what is due to them in form of money, recognition, appreciation and caring for their development is your Dharma. These are emotional wages that become due and must be paid without hesitation and in time! Reflect back each week to check if you have missed something.

Rakesh Saraf runs a company and like many the Covid shutdown impacted business. Faced with the emerging need to cut costs he chose to retain the employees rather than letting them go. He decided to move out of the swank Mumbai office to cut rental costs and got people to work from home. He did his Dharma well.

Clearing of dues, physical or emotional, lower than entitled is Adharma.

There can be others in the direct category depending on your circumstance and unique situation.

TRANSIENT

Old parents: We discussed this at the outset of this chapter. One thing must be reemphasised. This is just not about food, safety, shelter or money.

Some needs are emotional. There are needs for social contact. In particular, there are needs for maintaining their dignity at all times and with full mindfulness of the same. All these are your Dharma when such time comes.

When one starts thinking just only in terms of legal responsibility or of justifications or of comparisons, the gateways to Adharma open out. Dharma is never a mere exchange of dues in a cold calculated way.

Short term roles: These are the ones where you have said yes to something. You do what is needed and the element moves out from your second circle.

Meeting expectations and completing in time is your Dharma. At times you may feel indebted to someone and do things beyond the mere call of duty, which is fine as long as you do not go overboard.

Excessive lingering, not stepping out when done, extending, mismanaging, delaying without reason is Adharma. As was mentioned earlier not saying 'no' can also become Adharma.

Saying 'yes' for personal show off, some ulterior negative motive or for mere ego reasons is Adharma.

Walk-in's from your outer circles.

A friend falls ill, needs help, this person may for a short period enter your second circle. The minute the problem is resolved, the help is given, the friend moves back to an outer circle.

While dealing with others there should be no lies involved, if they are then the path is of Adharma.

Attending to a call for help, when your help will not endanger any inner circle or direct element is your Dharma.

It should be noted that the 'call for help' may be an actual ask by someone or arise from your judgement of the situation and circumstance. So all elements, direct or indirect, should be on your radar.

Not answering that call, when you could have, is Adharma.

Having said that, one should keep in mind the 'cost' of that call to help.

Is it short term, event-based, or is the call to help for a longer-term and greater responsibility? Here you must squarely judge if you accept then what/any (self) first circle damage or denial to a second circle direct element can take place. Then weigh the odds. Maybe reduce your help to the phase just to overcome an immediate crisis and not set expectations beyond or say no to the call and not set up false expectations. Many times when we get started then we do not reflect much, and we persist more than we normally should.

The question of 'sacrifice' appears here. Most times we do sacrifice something, the question to be asked always is what that sacrifice will cost you and whether you can afford it in terms of denial to some priority in your dharma circles. Minor sacrifices of course are different.

Costs in the short run and long term must be thought of. Money, time, effort, emotions, stress and risks – all should be factored in.

IN & OUT

This class is usually event-based. They are calls that need you to do something transactionally. They come, you do what is needed, then they move out of the circle. They can be simple, complex and even sometimes critical.

One special type of action also resides in this arena. Humankind has been generous and benevolent. This has been something that, without obligation to do, we do things that help others.

This is different from a situation where you have taken up a responsibility to do things that have sustained engagement and even that some responsibility falls on your shoulders due to some circumstance.

It is more of the one-off acts of kindness to provide that helping hand, often without any expectation of returns, many times without a formal ask for help from others. This is good Karma!

Returning a favour is another example of the in and out kind of situations.

CONFLICTS

As may be obvious by now there will be situations where you may be undecided, the brain tells you one thing, and the heart tells you another. At times, your brain tells you more than one option! It can also be that you cannot make a choice.

One of the primary purposes of the *7CircleDharma* is to help you have better decision making at times of dilemmas. This *7CircleDharma* provides you guidance on what takes precedence and helps you think through situations. It helps you define your priorities.

The governing principle is that damage must not be caused to a prior circle and any act that denies the 'rights' of a preceding circle priority is Adharma.

I use the word damage, this means that rights are not absolute, they can be diluted clearly in situations where a pause, a lower level than normal will not have high impacts in the medium to long term. Yet sometimes a casual approach is really the problem. We need to think through. Pause and reflect or a detailed work through as the situation demands.

Short term impacts should not be the ones that govern you in dilemmas unless have some compelling urgency or if they end up causing lasting damage to an inner circle demand. You can for example make up the gap of a temporary pause. Or you may decide to do something just out of a good gesture done.

Another aspect in dilemmas is going onto the why of the external demand on you. What are the purposes behind the ask of the other? These clearly should have no connects to negative aspirations or pursuits of the other.

Is your help being asked that will help the other unjustly dominate, manipulate, abuse or coerce others? Will it lead to the denial of some rights to others? Then even if that person appears to be dependent on your help your Dharma is to say NO because of the negatives associated.

So, one must judge what will your helping the other result in not just as the visible transaction but beyond into the purposes and situations and constructs at the recipients end.

Of course, the dilemmas do not exist for minor help and asks, so go ahead and do what your heart says!

Let me give you an example. A child asks for a toy, and the purpose of ask is that child will be happy and get some joy.

Then again, the child has many toys to play with and asks for another one. Maybe (s)he is just tired of the ones that are there and the purpose is a type of quest for change to discover something new.

In a further situation, this ask for another is more frequent and persists time and again. Now the purpose appears to be greed, possibly seeds of manipulations. Yes, there will be joy, happiness, discovery attached in this case too, but an overriding pattern that displays negative behaviour also stands out.

So do look at the purposes behind the ask particularly in situations where persistent demands on you are called upon.

Helping others, dependent on you or otherwise, if that leads to any support to a negative aspect is Adharma.

Oh, the list of negatives is endless, coercion, anger, inflated egos, cruelty, extortion, violence, cheating, manipulation, revenge, exploitation, falsehoods – there are many and these are usually visible if you stop and think. The key question is: Why? This uncovers it all.

In matters of importance or long-term commits, you may well need to ask a series of 'whys' to uncover the real purpose behind things.

A one-time benefit of the doubt is advisable in case you cannot come to a proper conclusion for minor matters this prevents you from being too judgemental. But if done, do closely watch what unfolds so that you learn as well as desist a future call on you for a repeat.

The ask, its purposes and consequences should become an automated approach to your thinking. While learning to do this it is a good idea to look back at your past actions, and dispassionately, analyse the ask-purpose-consequence triad and learn from it. From today's vantage point and plenty of hindsight, it is easier to learn and tune your mind.

Another aspect needs a mention. The children you have, dependent on you are fully in your 2nd circle. Once they gain capability on being on their own, they should not be forced to remain in your second circle and when they so desire and have the capability to manage, they should be permitted to do their own thing. It means that you have to be able to disconnect, material and physical aspects, and lingering on may impact their 1st circle development to potential.

Of course, emotional aspects do remain in the 2nd circle. A kind of cleavage occurs. The love/respect/emotion strands will remain, and the material aspects move out to another circle.

Inheritance: There is one curious kind of inheritance we can get from our parents in some instances. Apart from what they gave us, many good things, some skews can be produced because of the transferred desires of things they could not achieve in their lifetimes. Other things can be the missions they pursued and the entities that they set up.

These set up some invisible expectations for us to continue or to complete beyond their lifetimes. It can also happen that your personal Vision conflicts with these. There will be imperatives that play based on values you subscribe to, damage caused or otherwise, to what and why and for whom is all that important. You have to protect your first circle; you have to decide: adjust or not. What then is your Dharma?

The path is clear if you can see it! But you will need to work it out and take a conscious decision to be or not to be. Progressing just on momentum of the expectation, without the thinking through can lead to Adharma.

Sometimes the demands exist even in the current lifetimes. I have a nephew who got his medical degree when he passed out of Medical College and qualified as a doctor. With that degree in hand, he went to his father and said, 'I have become a doctor just as you wanted me to be, asked me to become to fulfil your dream'. His father gave a response full of pleasure and congratulated his son.

Then my nephew says, 'I have done what you said, fulfilled your dream, now may I continue my life as I want to?' Puzzled, he was asked, what do you want. Nephew says, 'I do not want to be in the medical profession, I want to prepare to get enrolled in the top management institute in India and make that my profession.

He did finally do that, passed out of the very best business school in India, the Indian Institute of Management, Ahmedabad and now is living his life the way he wants to, and successfully I may add in every sense.

Do be careful of what you compel others to do or insist upon.

Dependants mean that they may be dependent on you for

time, money, effort, affection, actions, guidance and such like, primarily anything that adds to their welfare and well-being. It aids their progress in life, though they may be dependent on you in some ways, yet they are in reality independent entities with their own dreams, vision and aspirations

It does not mean that you compel and abuse the dominant level you get into as their benefactor. Their freedom of choice has to be respected and responded to as befits their relative level of maturity, always best done with a gentle heart.

HIERARCHY

So far, the first circle is at the top, as long as the focus is to build your capability to deliver good Dharma.

Within the gaps between the circles, imagine it to be a wide band, some elements exist in the region near the inner circle and some things reside outward on the edges of this band touching the next outer circle. It is this band that defines the circle imperatives.

Within the band, thus, will be inner planets and outer planets and transients that passage across the band.

The inner ones, the direct elements, in normal situations, take precedence.

So, say an ask for money by someone who is currently dependent on you, a friend perhaps, and has transited in because of expectations set up due to a good friendship. Perhaps clearly is the purpose of the ask is say to buy a new mobile, and the person has a good functioning mobile, then this ask is not a dire need, and should be exported back out of the second circle.

Do note that when someone asks for help, they are knocking at the doors of your second circle. So, hear out you must but say yes and admit only after reflection, as once you say yes they enter your second circle.

On the other hand, this friend has a mobile that has stopped working, the absence of a device will prevent and impact his working, then the need is high, purpose and consequence clear. And the friend truly does not have the money to buy that mobile.

But wait, if your child needs a new laptop as (s)he is not coping with the work from home school work and you can spend on this laptop or the mobile, what will you do?

Obviously, the child you have is a direct element in the second circle and the friend is in an outward circle, the Dharma is clear. And, of course, if you get swept by emotion and do otherwise then clearly will be Adharma on your child.

Hierarchy is not only between the inner circle and the outer circles, but also where the issue lies within the inner band and outer band of the circle.

Having discussed all the above another aspect must be talked of as empathy is a vital dimension. There is logic and there are feelings that exist.

Eventually the 'how' you do is also hugely important besides the 'what' you do. Sometimes communication has an important role here as opposed to silently act. For example, whatever you say can be hard, soft, jocular, emotional, even sad in its expression. You may say something and yet your body language says something else!

The key is the right way at the right time and a good sidewalk to hug is, never with anger. Learning to say no with empathy is the solution. Listening and understanding situations are the keys only then you will practice good Dharma.

A long time back I came across something very interesting and I truly do not remember where I read it or who wrote it. This has a direct connection, so read on as near as I can remember it, though I have practised it often.

"If you are going to do something and there is some lingering doubt in your mind, then go into a corner, shut your eyes and say, "God, I am going to do xxx, will you be happy?"

The answer comes instantly, loud and clear from your heart. Try it!

CHAPTER 4

THE THIRD CIRCLE
THE PROVIDERS

Honour your commitments with Integrity
~ Les Brown

Each one of us has a vocation, a calling that you pursue. This may be your own business; it may be that you work for someone or some organisation. The calling you pursue, the business your run, the person/ entity you work for provide you with some kind of financial compensation and benefits in exchange for your services and work you do. This is what the third circle is about.

So, the words, economic profit (organisation) and financial profit (organisations as well as the individual) become the value exchange for the work you do.

You may also be involved in some work that derives social profit yet associated with that (or a third source) is something that provides you financial sustenance.

These rewards you get provide the sustenance to run your affairs, to buy things, to travel, to pay your bills, to amass wealth, to provide you with a status of dignity and respect and a host of other things that this money you earn provides you.

This, third circle, bolsters, sustains your first circle and a dent in this circle directly affects your capability to do things. It has a huge and direct bearing on the strength and empowerment of your first circle. Thus, 'the providers - the *annadata*' is placed as the third circle.

Annadata means provider.

Whatever entity, business, vocation, role, pursuit provides for you is your annadata. It provides the fuel in your tank!

Focus on this circle is important as the time you have on this planet has also to be used in gainful, productive and worthwhile pursuits.

Coming to others, whose main pursuit in life may not be a business or professional pursuit therein. They may work for NGO's, do social work, political or religious service.

Each one of them have also to live their lives and have some financial capability. Whatever the fountainhead that provides them with this capital or platform is also their *annadata.* They are unique as they not only have some source of financial profit but also social profit. Multiple *annadatas* can exist in that sense!

DIRECT

Your job: In reality, these two words have several contexts. It can mean delivering what you are meant to deliver to your manager and customers.

It may mean doing all that well enough to deliver to stakeholder expectations, to the owners of the business.

It may mean that you work excellently so that you not only retain your job as also flourish in your career paths.

It also has contexts that are already promoted into your second circle in terms of exercising authority and your responsibilities towards all who are dependent on you in any way within the professional context.

It will have connects that get into your first circle in terms of your needs for self-development, the development of your technical, functional and interpersonal skills. The acquiring of a role model personality and a positive character and the need to be continuously evolving in this changing world.

In short, it is also about working to your potential as this is the significant work arena where potential is played out.

Delivering all these consistently is your Dharma.

Your Business: There will be some who are entrepreneurs and the business they run is their *annadata*. Others work for some organisation or entity and are charged with operating the business or playing significant roles in such.

Obviously building and sustaining the business so that it has current and future economic payoffs is one strand in the thread.

So payoffs not only in the current period, then also scanning the horizon for emerging situations and aligning, adjusting to growing into future payoffs. Sort, medium and long run as they say!

Doing what needs to be done ethically and adhering to the laws of the land is another aspect. Leading, managing or serving it well is also the call. Delivering the expected value to your customer. All such and related are your Dharma.

Developing the business to its potential, seeking and seizing new opportunities and evolving to match the change around us also become prime needs. This evolving has to be timely as you continuously face a changing world.

This business not only provides you sustenance as also wealth, both materially move into your first circle. On occasions, this wealth may be redeployed into the business so doing so timely and wisely is also a call.

Your Customers: For a large number of aspects related to customers they may have moved into your second circle as they are dependent on you to deliver. Yet beyond the delivery of goods and/or services, as the case may be, several other things are important.

The quality, timeliness of what you deliver define the success of your business and its longevity.

The game is creating value and exchanging the value for a profit with a constant striving for an ethical above-average profit.

The ecosystem: The entire ecosystem that surrounds the third circle fits in here; the suppliers, the customers, the people, the processes, the infrastructure, the production and the delivery mechanisms are all things that need your attention.

There will be suppliers who need fair and valued partner treatment and not be taken for granted and positions of power not abused.

The people you serve, the people who serve you, it is retaining a positive, proactive, happy resonance with all that always matters.

Preventing waste of all types and growing your business is a consistent narrative. This also means managing your wealth, large or small, in personal possession or managed via the business are aspects you need to care about.

One of the biggest wastes we make, many times unconsciously, is that of our time. It is something, once spent, that is gone forever. Incredible as it may sound most of us waste a lot of time and one of your greatest Dharma is to invest/spend your time in the right things and prevent it from being stolen by meaningless activity.

A thumb rule to remember, if you work 8 hours a day, then it means those 8 hours are for work purposes only and diverting them, in that defined work period, into casual social media or unrelated to work activity is Adharma. We must reflect well before saying I am not like that. Even minutes count, and we waste these without realizing it!

Your several roles in the business: Being accountable for your responsibilities is one primary aspect.

Exhibiting good leadership, deploying a positive personality, motivating others, planning well, being organised, managing your commitment, leading into the future and while doing all that and more, retaining honesty and integrity and a sense of fair play, being of service to others and building trust are some of the other calls on you in terms of what your calling demands of you.

Matching all such expectations is your Dharma.

TRANSIENT

There may be calls made on you that are beyond the normal call of duty. These may be due to external circumstance or may come about as you exit steady-state operations into seizing a new opportunity or enlarging the existing. It may also be there as some crisis erupts.

As the pace of life increases so does the turbulence and these calls will come thick and fast often from unsuspected, undiscovered or unmanaged directions. Handling these always presents a level of risk and mitigating, minimising or pre-empting such is a constant call. To handle all this well is your Dharma.

These usually will last for a short period, often many of these may well become transient onto your second circle.

At times of normalcy even seeking any upgrades or improvements in the existing systems may add on extra work effort. Having used the word 'normalcy' a caution here. Normalcy now is an evolving dimension and should be thought of as getting back to near normal in any current situation as old normal are a dangerous place to stay.

Future projects, customer urgencies, market conditions all can have inroads in the transient arena.

We have seen in the current times a Tsunami of disruption caused worldwide by the Covid pandemic. When such transients come, they may last for quite some time, they uproot and unsettle in gigantic proportions and you have no choice but to run the gauntlet. The world meantime has changed into a new pattern. Evolving towards that, while managing the turbulence is a part of your dharma. Even if that means reinventing yourself.

In a way, these transients are usually projects that come your way as opposed to other responsibilities that last for longer durations.

IN & OUT

As is obvious the movement out is not always to an outer circle. It may just mean that it is moving out of that circle

Many times, the transients will call upon you to take on additional short term responsibility and migrate inwards to your second circle.

Variable demands by customers may come in and out even for a few day durations.

Resolving issues, sorting out ambiguity, listening to vendor requests, regulatory demands, managing expectations can be valid in this context.

CONFLICTS

One typical conflict is widely visible. The work-related time demands which eat into your personal time slots. This work-life balance issue is prevalent.

Curiously, it may be due to a skew in your mindset that has given precedence to this third circle demand over a second circle need and you get fixated on your business/career at the cost of your personal life. This is Adharma.

It is common to pop up justifications and explanations on why you do this. The argument raised is that 'I am doing it so that I bolster my first circle so that I can fulfil the needs of the second circle'. If I earn more money in my business or earn more salary, get promoted and earn even more, I am really doing it so that I can then fully give to the other people dependent on me and fulfil their wishes. Thus, goes the common story people tell themselves.

The counterfactual position is this: Your 6-year-old who needs to spend time with you now will grow up and today's time will not come again. Your first and second circle is just not money, we have seen it has other perspectives and dimensions and they get cheated off.

Having said that, most people miss a simple solution. Most of us grow up into very inferior management of how we spend our time. Most people misdirect time, they have no clarity on what actually the most appropriate time is to be spend in their roles.

A huge number of us grow up trying to do everything ourselves and not building others and using them to do the work.

Mostly we may not be experts in managing time rather we may have become experts in mismanaging time.

People have a fear of delegation and lack of belief in others, perhaps they even do not believe in their own capability to run things efficiently and effectively. This fear gets them to try and do everything themselves and prevents growth and they touch boundaries of what they can do.

It is entirely possible for the average person to do things more efficiently do more in less time. I have personally, in my vocation, helped thousands of people, managers, leaders, businesspeople do whatever they had been doing, perhaps even more, in a couple of hours less each day. Freeing up their time to do attend to their second and first circle imperatives.

So, I speak with authority in this type of conflict, borne of practical knowledge and experience of such matters.

Mismanaging your time is the greatest Adharma you can do to yourself and others around you. Its impacts cross over into many circles.

The other conflict in the third circle is caused by a lack of empathy. Empathy is the glue that connects humans. It is the magic that builds relationships. Lack of empathy automatically causes disconnects. It also is directly connected to the level of warmth or coldness in relations.

Of particular interest is your empathetic dealings with team members, customers, vendors – these will have a direct impact on performance.

One other conflict I must mention here. In your organisation, as you reach higher levels of authority there is a great need to exhibit trusteeship. The balance between personal and collective erupts time and again.

You have a fiduciary responsibility to balance between the

organisation gain and personal gain. Many of the scandals we read of are people who have failed the trusteeship and done great Adharma. As the greed negative replaces the integrity and honesty values the war is lost. One has to engage continuously to fight off an Adharma attack. More on this at the end chapters.

Finally, one more conflict exists and that is due to mindsets. Problem centric or solution centric. Mastering this as well as other positives is your Dharma.

Strive for harmony. Strive for balance. Strive for solutions. Strive to lead well in whatever roles you play. Strive to evolve into a better you as you pursue to perform your duty in the third circle.

The call will always be upon you to take up greater personal role ownership of whatever role you play. This results in greater focus and higher results as also helps you seize more opportunities.

Striving to be more efficient and effective is another pursuit. Uncover and reduce gaps between organisational potential and performance besides your own gap in such aspects is also a constant call to duty. You may also be called upon to develop others and ensure greater coordination and collaboration.

The capability section in the first circle has a great role to play here in your professional pursuits.

Seeking such things and proactively doing what needs to be done is your Dharma.

The providers sustain you and not letting them down is your Dharma.

CHAPTER 5

THE FOURTH CIRCLE
DEFENDING THE PLACE ONE LIVES IN

Ask not what your country can do for you,
Ask what you can do for your country
~ John F. Kennedy

The country you live in provides social order, security and you live in harmony with other citizens. It also provides you, varying from country to country, welfare schemes and other mechanisms to protect the country, its values, its progress, its assets and its citizens.

The economic redistribution of wealth by governments also contributes to healthcare, education and many other welfare measures apart from investments; all focusing on providing you, the citizen, an incrementally better quality of life.

Thus, doing your duty as a citizen is a prime area of Dharma. Paying your taxes, not crossing legal or regulatory boundaries, not encroaching on other people's rights, not causing harm to others, aiding peaceful coexistence and suchlike, all are your Dharma.

Anything that degenerates the existing systems, boundaries or wellbeing becomes a threat to you and others. Protecting it is your Dharma.

Your role as an individual in this mass community and geography is the key concern of the 4th circle.

Coming to the aid of your country and its constituents at times of threat is also a major call on your Dharma. Be it rain, flood, riot, pandemic, natural calamity, times of war; all will call upon you to contribute beyond your normal call of duty. Doing this, to the best of your ability, is your Dharma.

A key to understanding this call is, 'That when you could have done you did not shy away from doing so'. Your acts could be by active contribution, direct or indirect, major or minor or just by a public expression of solidarity.

There are other contexts one must think of.

It is not nations that fail, it is actually the people leading such countries that fail – as also people who empower such leaders to remain in power. This may describe an individual dictator or even some elected representative or a person seizing power by force or a series of such and their cohort.

The *Rig Veda* describes the duties of a king:

'The main work of a king was the protection of its subjects. The king should have the best conduct, should have the noblest virtues. Should be well read, nourish his subjects and protect the state.; should punish the culprits and retain firmness of purpose, should honour good persons contribute to the progress of the state and is advised to help the weak and helpless people.'

Contexts and the meaning of the above are much similar today – perhaps in a much sharper and enlarged multidimensional detail.

The essence of what was written is in the very first sentence and has an outward focus towards the people of the country.

Today the 'king' would be replaced by an elected person and be assisted by a team of ministers – all of them should follow the ideal. It may also include dictators or people who have wrested power, who sadly may ignore the call.

Even functionaries in governance positions below should adhere to, in the subset of their responsibilities, the principles of duty and legal/regulatory aspects. If you happen to be anywhere in this ecosystem, then the primacy of the country needs is your Dharma while executing your official duties. If the fiduciary responsibility is breached and all roads lead to Adharma.

One sees a lot of abuse and misuse of power which of course is Adharma done by the one who abuses and the ones who abet.

The *Rig Veda* also talks of the duties of citizens (subjects). It is the duty of the subjects to make a right and virtuous person the king. So even as you cast your vote, the Dharma starts right there.

Nations also have values. These may be spelt out in some declaration or constitution. Also, many may be reflected in traditions. So, there are a core set of values for each nation and when these positive values are abundantly practised nations rise and the populace benefits in many ways.

Examples of such nation type values can be freedom of speech, equality, democracy, peace, growth, prosperity etc. What we know as democracy has roots in ancient Greece, where the laws centuries ago, were primed to secure the life and property of society as opposed to protecting a select group or leader or other persons. This has been the source of most modern democratic thought. Different countries will express it differently. Trying to reverse the primacy of societal gain in favour of a person, group or elite has been the primary cause of strife and Adharma.

In India, *Ahimsa* (non-violence), equality, harmony, tolerance, compassion and freedom have been used. In the USA Independence, rights to life, liberty and pursuit of happiness, equality, diversity, unity and individualism have been used. France has liberty, equality and fraternity. Kenya has patriotism, unity, rule of law, democracy, non-discrimination, dignity, justice, equity and inclusiveness. The UK has democracy, rule of law, individual liberty, mutual respect, tolerance of those of different faiths and beliefs.

As would be obvious many of these apply to every country, some are spelt out, some are by tradition. So, a national spirit exists. Mahatma Gandhi says, 'A national spirit is necessary for national existence'. Thus, any personal agenda that deflects away will dent the national spirit and existence. Thus, defending also means defending national identity.

What is obvious here is that irrespective of the personal priorities of values you hold and practice in the context of your personal agendas, there is a clear and overriding call on your behaviour when you pursue national agendas. You as an individual may not have the absolute right to override the national values. These are the constituents of the national spirit.

Not failing the nation is your Dharma.

Each new leader of a country has personal values. These actually will be values professed in his or her individual capacity or by and through his/her dominant ideology. Many times, these may clash with the core values of the nation. Sometimes just causing a minor skew or a move away within a band of tolerance. There are times the personal or ideological values can overtake and override the nations core values. Conflict results invariably in such cases.

Of course, many times the personal/ideological values may be in near full alignment or to a core minimum level.

In dictatorial regimes the personal values, often inter spiced with a lot of negatives, thus themselves become the temporary, usually disastrous core of the nation for some period of time.

There will be debates on political philosophies that may arise, but the core of all good ones is well being of citizens, enhancements of citizens, safety and security of the nation, prosperity, dignity, respect, welfare, opportunity, progress, education and health types of imperatives. There may be more such. Lastly and most importantly there is a universal need in remaining free of strife and violence. The approach may differ, but the principles concern the most valid and desired outcomes which remain common.

Our focus is on how the individual behaves in whatever be the circumstance.

The place you live in, thus in clear context, means the country you live in. From the point of view of a map, it has geographic boundaries that define its expanse. Yet there are a host of issues that connect and remain interconnected. A complex mix, amongst these, religion, colour, economy, philosophies, culture, arts, ambitions, region, race are just a tiny few that complete the whole.

Given all that, each country has to be managed and governed by people.

At the helm of affairs would be a principal person, designated as head of state, and others who are all committed to a particular ideology or a mix of several. These people at the helm are persons with great authority, power as well as responsibility. They set the agendas. They move in specific directions. Their one act of Dharma or Adharma gets magnified immensely in its impact as it affects a very large number of people directly or indirectly.

Yet the world has seen, and history gives repeated proof of this, that ambitions of individuals play a great part in how it actually shapes up. In extreme situations stands taken by some have resulted in wars causing destruction, death and turmoil severely impacting the rights of millions of people. The same is also true for the bitter internal conflicts within countries as factions get polarised and run into violent conflict.

Thus, for persons in those positions of human governance persisting on imbalanced personal negative agendas causes great Adharma. If violence is occurring, or even appearing to be possible, it is a sure sign that some negative forces are at play.

Another very important perspective emerges. A person in the position of human governance has also to observe 'Social Dharma' as a prime outlook in conducting his or her role. This means that the person has to replace his YOU 1st Circle primacy, while playing the role of human governance, by the 'US' statement becoming the 1st Circle in his/her public capacity. This US includes then the collective welfare of all individuals as well as the values of the nation.

The nation in fact becomes the first circle owner and not the person. This is a test where many leaders fail.

In the preamble and Article 1 of the Universal Declaration of Human Rights this is stated with great clarity;

'Disregard and contempt for human rights have resulted in barbarous acts which have outraged the conscience of mankind, and the advent of a world in which human beings shall enjoy freedom of speech and belief and freedom from fear and want has been proclaimed as the highest aspirations of the common people. All human beings are born free and equal in dignity and rights.'

These are the founding principles in your role in Social Dharma and the basis on which the collective US based 1st circle is formed.

Relating to the context of the *7CircleDharma* you can either be a direct contributor to the governance of your nation or a citizen in it. In each role the primacy of the declaration forms the principles you must adhere to – that becomes your overriding Dharma.

One can be active or passive, yet causing, initiating, sustaining, ignoring, abetting anything that goes against the grain of these rights and the national spirit is Adharma. Passively standing by and just observing or even avoiding is also not good, do what you can while also respecting your personal 1st circle safety.

Another aspect must be mentioned here, many places of this world have elected governments and while voting for those representatives it is your Dharma not to get abusers or manipulator of power elected.

Assist, protect, uphold, contribute, maintain peace and harmony are words and values that are strongly associated with the 'place you live in'. Do your bit, insignificant as it may seem, that is your Dharma. This part of social dharma is to be practised even at the individual level.

DIRECT

Country: This has been explained above and is the prime facet concerning your 4th circle. There are calls on you in normal times as also at a different level in times of minor as well as severe disruptions.

City: This is something that has immediate concerns on you, the city you live in work in, it may add elements beyond the larger picture. Obviously, there may be add on factors, beyond the nation-based imperatives at play, localised if you may, that need to be factored in. These actions add on rather than replace the national imperatives.

Locality: This can be your immediate neighbourhood, and as we move from a macro view of a country down to a micro view of the street(s) the type of behaviour you can exhibit changes and has a more direct connect to your day-to-day actions.

Peace: this has a special mention as living in, promoting and ensuring this is continuous demand on each one of us.

Taxes: paying these as due is a key aspect and evasion, avoidance is squarely Adharma.

Besides the above, there is a need to pay back to society and looking beyond yourself and contributing, when you can, is something you must try to do.

Staying always within the ambit of law is a prime demand, as also not manipulating or abusing legal processes.

There could be a host of other things, maintaining cleanliness and doing things that do not cause inconveniences or damage to others is a further call on you. In fact is the principal call on a leader.

Curiously many of us are aware of what ought to be done at an individual level but yet many fail to do what they have to do. This perhaps has also a reflection on national character and culture but not always so.

The covid pandemic offers a startlingly painful and vivid exhibition of our failings. The clear call on wearing masks, keeping social distancing and even getting vaccinated are things that the scientific community calls on us to do with clear reason and these are the things that ought-to-be-done. Many comply and don't resist, they do their Dharma.

One is aghast at the callous 'wont-wear-the-mask' types, the irresponsible behaviour in not maintaining social distancing and the illogical aversion and at times a downright stupid fight for not getting vaccinated. Whether they do it out of personal conviction or at the call of some influencer does not matter. Their Dharma gets impacted and all they end up doing is Adharma not only to themselves but also to others.

Periodically, therefore, one must revisit, sit back and look inwards into our habits of thought, attitudes, beliefs and locate those things that we need to change so that we can get on doing those things that we ought to be doing. Once you reflect and realise, then Act!

TRANSIENT

A major part of the transient arises out of abnormal situations, any disaster or disruption that threatens you and others around you from living their normal lives will put extra demands on you. This ' call to duty' of course will go away as the situation normalizes. But the question is always what you do in the moments of need.

The other transient aspect can be your level of response to situations. This will depend highly on your own individual situation and it is all right to do less than another when your circumstances prevent you.

An important transient comes up when you cast your vote. Do not be swept away by herd behaviour or influencers. Leaders are dealers of hope and they promise you future visions. At such times do look at their past performances!

Look for people who will do the greatest social good and

stand the test of the universal declaration. Voting for such people is your Dharma. Voting for ones who go against the grain is Adharma.

Of course, if all available options fit in the Dharma category, then choose as you deem fit.

Yet a sad truth these days is we have people who do not stand the test of truth and ethic.

The regret of 'I could have' or 'I should have' will give you pointers in the direction of Dharma.

IN&OUT

Interplays of your inner circles will cause you to move out and live your individual life, that is fine. These are normal time variations to which you adjust and align as long as you have your priorities right these movements will not fail you and cause no damage.

There are other times when the call to duty is much higher.

The nation also is just not vulnerable to external threats. It is also vulnerable to internal threats. When these threaten to destroy peace, harmony and well being then the scale and impact of such forces call on increasing demands on you as an individual.

War's result-arise from external countries, with boundaries, religions, people or philosophies clashing. One aspect is preventing escalation, however, when the battles are on, they must be fought.

Most times wars are primed by one Leader in a country mixing personal agendas into the national and coupled by huge influencing power borne out of an ability to rouse emotions or out of absolute unfettered power positions. They may also be primed by national agendas that seek to enlarge the country's sphere of influence and control.

When wars start there is no time for debate of who started

and why. In the midst of battle, it is only your actions of self-preservation and preservation of what you stand for that matters. The call of duty will be towards direct action and so must you do at such times. The call of duty for others may be support and expressing public solidarity. It is not a time for hibernation.

You may have conscription based on laws in force or demanded of you arising from self- protection imperatives. The call of duty rises and doing such duty is your Dharma.

The other conflicts are from within the country. In extreme, they may result in civil wars, in mass migrations as people escape to save their lives. Sadly, there have been many, from Rohingyas, to Syrian refugees to Pakistan instigated and sponsored exodus of Kashmiri Pandits. My apologies to ones that I did not name. there are so many who have suffered the indignity and loss. The sad part in the story are the people who just stood by and avoided doing Dharma.

The clear Adharma connects can be discovered behind these, things like; disowning a section of the populace, greed, cowardice, false assumptions, treating one part of the citizens as secondary, discrimination, lack of compassion – you name it!

Then there are conflicts that are unsettling, many times violent, and are fuelled again by individuals trying to impose their way and personal agendas into the nation. Many times, it is a manipulation of circumstances attempted for personal material gain or for ego fulfilment or even just the heady sense of power.

Most people want to live life as they want to, peacefully. The core of governance problems arises when an individual or a group of individuals at the helm of affairs, want you to live your life as they want you to. I demand you do as I say, this type of call made one way or the other, is the most abusive and disruptive. It negates the core value of freedom. It is intolerance to other views that creates rigidity. Is wrong when this impacts any freedom of others.

And when such demands, 'live as I want you to' is made by the person at the helm of governance the damage starts and the unrest. This is hugely disruptive as it moves beyond not just the national spirit but also the national constitution and laws in force.

I would like to share two quotes from Erich Fromm. In his book, Escape from Freedom:

'When Fascism came into power, most people were unprepared, both theoretically and practically. They were unable to believe that man could exhibit such propensities for evil, such lust for power, such disregard for the rights of the weak, or such yearning for submission. Only a few had been aware of the rumbling of the volcano preceding the outbreak...Escape from Freedom attempts to show, modern man still is anxious and tempted to surrender his freedom to dictators of all kinds, or to lose it by transforming himself into a small cog in the machine, well fed, and well clothed, yet not a free man but an automaton."

He also says in his book, Fear of Freedom:

We forget that, although each of the liberties which have been won must be defended with utmost vigour, the problem of freedom is not only a quantitative one, but a qualitative one; that we not only have to preserve and increase the traditional freedom, but that we have to gain a new kind of freedom, one which enables us to realize our own individual self; to have faith in this self and in life.

In the words of Carl Jung: The most dangerous things in the world are immense accumulations of human beings who are manipulated by only a few heads.

At the end what you do or do not do is all that matters in

these constructs. It is your personal behaviour and taking personal responsibility that are of concern.

Not being manipulated is your ultimate Dharma.

CHAPTER 6

THE FIFTH CIRCLE
ALL THOSE KNOWN TO YOU

You create your own universe as you go along.
~ Winston S. Churchill

The fifth circle is about people you know. People you have met physically or virtually.

These can be different relationships. Your immediate family, your relatives, some old friends, some new ones. Beyond these will be acquaintances - professional or personal.

Yet others may be there who you do not know personally yet some connection exists in as much as they are not unknown entities. They may be people who are involved in social work, religious entities, government functionaries.

A remoter aspect, but still at the fringes of the fifth circle band would be political or social figures whose calls you resonate with and have the potential to influence you. They may be unmet, even remote, but do create a surprisingly high impact on how you think and act priming emotional forces that override the logical ones.

There are also people from fraternities, clubs, associations that could be included in this fifth circle.

Any bond due to some connections can draw people into the fifth circle. Any shared event, person, entity or connection can draw them in.

The Dharma is to do as much as you can to meet their expectations, physical, social or emotional however not at the cost of some inner circle. Adharma is to create, maintain an unhealthy disconnect.

This 5th circle band is wide as it can range from immediate family to a fraternity member or even a connection on social media. You must nurture the quality of the relationship and not allow it to degenerate as far as possible.

The quantum of what you can do, the frequency of your doing so, the intensity of engagement will of course vary.

Emotional Aspects

All people have emotional needs. Your parents, your children, your siblings, your spouse – all are in the inner band of your fifth circle and their emotional needs must be met. In fact, this band of immediate relations exist dually in your 2nd and 5th circles. A never to be forgotten rule is that for their emotional needs, they are still in the 2nd circle and for most other aspects in the 5th circle.

As you move to the outer parts of this band the emotional needs are far less demanding, yet they do exist. Sometimes all it needs is some expression of word, act or deed that signals, 'I care'.

There will be times the people in your fifth circle are facing hardship or trauma, their level of emotional need will grow higher for a certain period of time. Bereavement of someone near to them is one example and is an emotional need that is transient but one where the silent demand to be fulfilled is high.

The whole ethos of humanity emerging out as a social species is based on the fact that we live together and there exists a weak or strong bonding. This bonding must be reinforced as needed, otherwise, we would simply be a herd of animals.

Having fun together, enjoying life is one of the most sought after and important aspects of our lives and this happens and gets expressed in the fifth circle. You just cannot have fun while sitting all alone!

Do what you can when the time comes, that is your Dharma. It may cost you time, energy or effort and such investment can always be made. Making excuses not to do veers to Adharma.

Stay connected

A person in the middle zone of your fifth circle may not have the same imperatives as those of close family. These people could be friends and relatives.

Personal traits and habits that have formed come into play. Some people develop into reticent beings, some the very opposite. How you behave becomes your personality. The good news is that behaviour can be changed, and better positive habits can be formed to alter your personality. With a desire to do, that does lurk in everyone, all it may need is setting up purposeful goals to change. The frequency of how often you reach out may not be as important as that you do reach out.

One more dimension is at play. Connect just does not mean that you call, meet and talk. It means you listen well; it means you have empathy and ask the right questions. Connect does not mean that you went and only talked about yourself – yes do that but allow the others to share. It implies a satisfying shared experience be it joy or sorrow or fellowship or fun not just for you but for the other too.

When you listen and understand only then you exhibit the 'I care' attitude. Of course, it goes without saying that the other must know that you care, just feeling inside of you is not enough.

Are there people you should stay connected with and haven't? Do you care about them? Do something! That is your Dharma.

The other question you must ask yourself is, does my interactions with others produce negative or positive feelings. What is my predominant pattern on who others perceive this to be? Once you identify then either grow the pattern or alter it.

Social Interaction

Would one of your prime needs be to have an enjoyable life? To do things that give you pleasure. Sure, both of these would be your first circle elements, sure some things you may enjoy in solitude, yet most are in the company of others. They will remain incomplete with an incomplete level of social interaction!

Similarly, your children, your spouse, your aged parent or elder, who may be in your second circle, they too derive pleasures of life if they interact with others. Your situation may provide you with decisions that say yes or no to these needs.

Denying them the adequate opportunity is Adharma. Denying yourself social interaction opportunity is also Adharma.

Yes, there has to be a balance. Whatever the interaction efforts cost in terms of time, effort or even money, you must weigh the impact of that spend on your other circle priorities. In some instances, it is ok to give in to your heart!

The fact is that overdoing anything can be bad, which means that if your time, effort or money costs have a large impact or damage any primary circle need then it will be Adharma.

Physical v/s virtual

The world has changed and so have our capabilities. This has been happening all the time across ages. However now the restraints of a physical nature dissolve and diffuse with the advent of new technology and its expressions. Especially the internet and mobile along with the multitude of apps and other things. Many of us are so avid users that we touch our mobile or other device an average of every 5 minutes!

Here are opportunities that many seize and use effectively to generate a greater connect within the 5th Circle and band within. It costs much less time, money, energy as the virtual shatters physical and geographic boundaries.

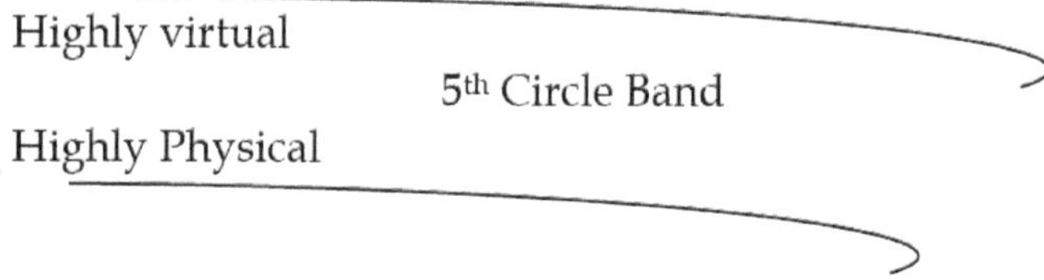

One may be tempted to think that the 5th Circle band exists in two distinct shades, one is more physical towards the inner edge and the outer edges more virtual. While the physical can use virtual tools, the virtual members do occasionally migrate to the inner band boundaries of physical interactions.

The precedence of Dharma is always towards the inner border of the circles yet do keep in mind that there are also movements within the band.

Having said that, a startling realisation that, perhaps primed by the emerged conditions, I have a few people who now I know very well, interact weekly, have had quality conversations but have never met in person face to face. The pandemic year has forced many into faster adoption and usage. So don't wash off the virtual world so easily!

The virtual world has an awesome power to add people to your fifth circle. There are exciting possibilities that arise due to this. Irrespective of young or old the reality of this virtual world expanding out and becoming more and more important in our lives is a fact that cant be ignored. As they say, a whole new world exists there!

The virtual has now gained another power that is to directly impact your social image and reputation. Many of us share posts, tweets or information over the digital medium. We put in our likes or otherwise expressing opinions as we do. We have virtual profiles that we set up and these matter too on what people perceive you as.

Many of us may have thousands of connections enlarging their 5th circle further to unimaginable limits, at times enlarging further to become influencers. As we grow in these numbers our capability to influence and impact others increases.

Which brings us to an interesting fact. Spreading rumours, disinformation and negativity is squarely Adharma. This does mean situations when done deliberately. Many times this is fed by a tendency in all humans that is to enjoy a bit of gossip and without realising we may spread the wrong story around, so be a bit careful.

Seek sources of happiness

We, humans, seek several things in life. These could be money, possessions, position, power, recognition, growth and suchlike. They are all fine at a given situation of your life and do what you can to enhance and overcome circumstance to achieve.

Yet, if you reflect, whatever we do we are doing so to have some kind of contentment and satisfaction. This word - satisfaction, can have two aspects. Dissatisfied or Unsatisfied. Apart from indicating that you are not satisfied, they indicate the nature of the situation as it exists. Dissatisfied implies you want less of that situation; you want to escape out of it. Unsatisfied means you want more fulfilment of the situation and do not want to escape out of what you are doing.

Having said that the pursuit of contentment is an unending journey. Yet nebulous as it may be yet milestones exist, accomplishments are done, and these give you pleasure and happiness. Thinking, 'at the cost of what?' is a shadow that walks with it!

Contentment is variable. It is always in flux. There are times when one gets these urges inside and one gets into a disturbed state somewhat agitated inside even you might have felt perfectly comfortable moments back.

Persisting disturbed states of mind cause stress and this prevents your focus on some immediate needs. Getting back to a 'normal' state is always a prime imperative. Normal of course will vary from person to person! Yet the context here is in terms of a mind not in turmoil.

In India, as well as now in large parts of the world, meditation is often used as a tool to regain balance.

One type, for example, Vipassana meditation, helps you overcome anger, frustration and even grief. It helps normalise thinking when something desirable is not happening as also when something undesirable has happened. There may be many other types of meditation equally effective. I addition you may have other ways of finding peace of mind, use whatever that works for you, seek out those avenues.

To quieten your mind when agitated is your Dharma.

The best solution always is rooted in the fact that a shared moment of joy enhances and multiplies happiness. So do look out for and generate those shared moments with your fifth circle. Enthusiasm is always infectious so go ahead and catch it from someone!

Fraternities & Clubs

Joining such a group multiplies your opportunity and extends your fifth circle, At times these groups may relate to students or to professional pursuits, other times people just enjoy doing something together in a group, enjoy each other's company or even work towards a social cause.

I have been a member of Rotary International and being so was a very fulfilling experience in many dimensions. Rotary has multiple objectives. Fellowship at the core and I made many new friends, enjoyed their company, shared fulfilling times on common interests and partied too!

Yet the other face of Rotary is that of community service and through this avenue has made fantastic contributions to our communities by projects in several areas of need. Rotary International, through the Rotary Foundation, has been one of the largest contributors to the Global Polio eradication programs with investments of time and effort of Rotarians apart from over 2 billion USD in cash contributions.

So, if you can belong to one, large or small, you will extend your reach and improve the quality of your life and that of others.

Contribute to organisations you belong to

Many other organisations also exist that exist for professional work endeavours. As you join these you gain in your inner circles too. The most enriching part can be of contributing to their success by your effort, time, money or professional contributions.

There are many professional bodies, chambers, associations that help you grow in many ways as well as help you interact meaningfully.

Empower others

Of the multitude of people that can exist in your 5th Circle, you must look at ways you can enrich their lives and one powerful way is to work to empower them.

Many a time we bypass such opportunities, you will find several instances in your life where some guidance or other act can empower another person known to you.

Seizing such an opportunity and doing what you can is also your Dharma. Do not look away.

The bottom line: Do things that you can do which give happiness to you and to others, that is your Dharma. The art is doing this without impacting an inner circle element. And doing things for others will give you great joy when you do this.

There are many happy and fulfilling moments that you will find in the 5th circle.

CHAPTER 7

THE SIXTH CIRCLE
WHAT ABOUT THE REST?

My religion is very simple, my religion is kindness
~ Dalai Lama

The sixth circle has all the people living on this planet – the ones who do not have any direct connection with you.

They could be walking the street, live in another city, village or country. All human beings on this planet!

After you have done your dharma to the ones in your inner circles, and if you have the capability do more, then the sixth circle opens out.

If you have resources, can manage the effort and time, directly or through others, then the Dharma is to do something. Do note, resources just do not mean money, time also is a resource.

An example here would explain this. The Bill and Melinda Gates foundation may have no direct knowledge or connection of a person in a remote village in a different country. Yet through their contributions to their Sixth circle, innumerable doses of the polio vaccine have helped people stay polio-free and healthy. This extends to other causes they pursue as well notably the recent pledge of USD 10 billion towards vaccine development and for the world's poorest countries.

There are many others, Azim Premji in India is another such person. He was again the first in the India 2020 Philanthropy list with a top contribution of Rupees 79000 million. There are countless others large and small and each one has made a difference in their own way and to their capability. There are millions of school children who raise small amounts for various causes. Each drop fills the ocean.

They could help, they did help. That is, they did their Dharma.

Once you start looking beyond yourself you will find several things that can be done to help out others on this planet. There are many avenues. However, do think through how much time or resource you spend on such avenues and do not cause an imbalance in other circle needs to erupt.

We talk of Corporate Social responsibility (CSR) and in fact, may have many times a legal and regulatory obligation that companies need to comply with.

Wikipedia describes it thus: Corporate social responsibility (CSR) is a type of international private business self-regulation that aims to contribute to societal goals of a philanthropic, activist, or charitable nature by engaging in or supporting volunteering or ethically-oriented practices.

It must be noted that CSR is a business function of an enterprise with the objective to earn 'social profit' for the enterprise and its stakeholders. This is different from charities that may be charged solely with a mission and purpose of helping society or contributing to a social cause but have no other business purpose attached.

Having said that, what about Personal Social Responsibility? At the level of an individual.

All these, CSR, charities, causes, PSR align with Dharma values.

Should you give back to society? This question also needs to be asked without applying the lens of money. You can for example contribute by time and effort. The question you have to answer is, should you or should you not.

The what, the who, the how, the when and where are secondary. This is highly related to ones own nature and the choices we exercise.

What is your intent? The answer points you to your Dharma or Adharma.

CSR

If you head an organisation or are part of one that brings you into a position of influence or authority to do something about CSR. In some countries, you can have legal obligations to do something. Even if there is no legal compulsion, the fact is that you can contribute by setting up or support schemes or projects that help others.

It does not depend on the size of the organisation; even small companies can put something aside and contribute. This should come from your heart when you lead an entity!

Equality

How do you view others in a general sense? If we ask you, 'do you favour equality', the answer will be a quick yes in most people. The matter does not end with this answer!

Then if we ask you, 'have you practised this equality principle?' Do you, for example, treat boys and girls equally? Do you hold some gender bias, caste bias, poor-rich bias, or other such instances? There are a lot of places this inequality can lurk, and it is Dharma not to get entrapped in such patterns and break out.

Inequality can have two contexts. Of things you do and what things are in the context of situations that you connect with. Both are areas where you can do something about it by your thoughts and actions.

The macro view also exists and if you are in a position where you could help, advise or share, then do so and do not shy away.

Whenever you reach interface points between you and the other people, these are the points where doing actions arise. Whether the boundary approaches you or you approach the boundaries, that interface is where the call to dharma appears.

Freedom

Sometimes the surge from people you do not know appears as the populace fights against current or impending fears. The fear may be real, distorted or false.

At these times you may not be approaching the interface rather the interface boundary is expanding towards you. It may impact you and you may even join in.

So, the question arises, does a person have the freedom to do anything he/she likes? To what extent?

Freedom is just not about geographies and governance issues. Freedom, in reality, is sought from injustice, inequality, indignity, dominance, discrimination, inequities, ambiguity, imbalance, uncertainty, lawlessness and a host of other worries, anxieties and fears.

When the time comes to do your bit, the least you can do is to advocate, stand with others to overcome negative distortions.

Freedom comes with responsibility and as long as you do not cause damage to others, infringe on their rights you are in the space of Dharma.

APJ Abdul Kalam says: Any country is as good as its citizens; their values and their character will be reflected in the country's make-up.

No Discrimination

Many beliefs and convictions we hold may have roots in some kind of discrimination. Sometimes we do not even realise or be aware that we are discriminating. Such beliefs and convictions should be changed as they possess a basis of bias towards things or people.

Looking back frequently at our past actions is a great source of learning. Hindsight often throws up surprises. Periodically sit back for a moment and reflect, 'did I do anything which directly or indirectly in, say the past one month, that resulted in some kind of discrimination?'.

Dwell on this question and you may discover some things out of place. What is more important then is to think about how you could have done something different. This trains your inner self and helps you greatly to change future instances.

Seeking and reflecting upon the past, learning from it and then acting towards minimising future discrimination is your Dharma.

If you aid, abet, abdicate to discrimination - the action will come back to you. Reflect not just as a person, but for roles you play or the entities you lead. This habit of self-reflection makes you a better person.

Removing such points of discrimination as you may discover is your Dharma.

The destitute

There are many who are in misery or are in miserable states of existence. It may not matter what they did or did not do. They are in pain and unable to meet even the primary needs of survival and security. They may have made mistakes or have been hit by circumstance and it is their present state that is of import.

'This does not concern me', is a selfish thought so use the other one, 'What is it that I can do about it.'

Even small gestures surprisingly do help. You may of course help with money, and beyond that, there are clothes you do not use or other things that can be given away. Do not be cynical and give what you can. After you give, think again what more can I do!

'I have nothing to give', is always wrong. There is empathy – a kind word can always help. A smile bought on the others face is always something that will be good.

Refugees

Extending on the above, there are classes of people who have been driven out of their homes by some brutal, cruel thing that was so fearful that they had no choice but to flee.

To arrive at a strange place, with nothing in hand and nothing to look forward to. Such people deserve our compassion and help. Doing so is your Dharma, in a way they approach your 2nd circle. They are knocking at your door!

Having an open, caring and giving heart is called for in such situations.

Safety of others

You have the freedom to do anything. This comes with a responsibility that while you do what you want, it should not cause damage of any kind to others, expose them to danger or jeopardise their safety.

Any reckless or negligent act is Adharma.

Causes

People pick up things due to some resonance with the values they hold dear. They have the passion to highlight and pursue the issue to remove some imbalance.

Having said that, the world is full of imbalances!

You may not personally resonate with everyone and everything and the resonance can be strong or weak. Sometimes it may bother you and yet you can do nothing about it except perhaps feeling a bit sad.

If you feel deeply, are in a position to do something about it then go ahead and do it. If you could have then it ought to have been done is the key to remember.

Activists, by spaced repetition, can also influence you. These can be mostly slowly developed crests that you form and align with, using a mix of logic and feeling thinking.

Yet they can form quickly if you resonate well. Whether it is the #MeToo or #blacklives matter, our imagination and behaviour are captured towards what strongly resonates within. Influencers can pull your thinking towards things that support the test of dharma.

PS: there will be others in the world that do not concern you in any way, you may encounter many whether in need or otherwise. A good idea is to do whatever you can to <u>at the very least to respect the dignity of the other</u> and you will remain in safe positive zones.

CHAPTER 8

THE SEVENTH CIRCLE
NON-PEOPLE

The greatest threat to our planet is the belief
that someone else will save it
~ Robert Swan

Outside the sixth circle is planet earth. Anything and everything in here is also our concern. Viewed differently by different people perhaps, yet the imperatives exist. It could also extend out to places we reach our touch beyond the planet!

Our land, air, water, the trees and vegetation, the animals, the other aspects of our environment. We all have a responsibility towards all that.

The call is to do nothing that degrades the seventh circle or the call to minimise damage, can be the associated aspect of Dharma.

On one extreme end are things like the burning of forests, in one year for example over 3000 square miles were burnt up in the amazon. Some people estimate that by now 20% is gone, in 2020 over 30,000 fires were on in the amazon rainforest. Not only that host of fauna and flora, but indigenous tribes also have all been impacted. Similarly, the Living Planet report by the WWF shows that wildlife populations have plummeted by 68% since 1970.

There will be fine lines separating 'using' and 'degrading'. These are the exceptionally fine lines that we must respect. But the ones where there is no fine line and wanton destruction must be stopped.

Many times, the seventh circle will hover and enter into your inner circles as environmental damage occurs.

May be climate change, may be pollution… they no longer are in the seventh circle. They impact our lives directly.

India's National Capital Region has been facing very high levels of pollution impacting millions of lives. The situation gets worse in the autumn and winter months as additional climatic factors like low windspeed plugs in, however, the main source is from reckless and irresponsible stubble burning in neighbouring states as well as the pollution load from vehicles, and construction work.

As this directly impacts your health it moves directly into your first circle. So distant as the 7th circle may seem it can walk in anytime into your innermost circles and does so in many instances, pollution for example is a constant impact. There are many such which are of direct concern.

Then there is also a continuous battle between human led development and consequential damage.

Many of these things concerning the planet are interconnected. Global warming leads to alteration in rain patterns as the surface area of the sea increases. The evaporation disturbs air currents. Produces extreme weather conditions. It melts glaciers thus impacting the availability of freshwater. Warming arises from excessive emissions. This also led to impacts on the natural habitat of all living forms plants, animals, fish.

Apart from us, humans, the other things get impacted. Sea, Plants, animals, air, water, poles, deserts, minerals, rivers, forests, one can keep adding to the list and what is important as you name each one of these you will clearly see them in discomfort or disaster situations. There are contexts of being threatened, endangered, depleted, polluted, poisoned, and damaged.

Ecosystems, habitats have been exploited and to levels that threaten their sustainability.

We, humans, have grown in numbers, there has been rapid economic development and rising consumption. The populations and needs will also keep growing. This we cannot change. What we can change is however our levels of responsibility on what and how we do. We can change our actions.

David Attenborough once said, perhaps to educate us; If we disappeared overnight, the world would possibly be better off. We do need other kinds of solutions though!

Then personal agendas emerge. We can reduce consumptions. We can re-use, we can recycle, we can refuse some, plastic, for example, this calls for behaving responsibly.

These are in the span of each individual's control, so it is your Dharma to reduce, recycle and refuse things that damage the circle.

Apart from the above we can educate others, contribute in terms of effort, money or even time to help conservation or any other cause that you gel with.

Above all, we can control what we say and do. Don't waste is a powerful mantra. Ultimately it all boils down to what we do as individuals.

Personally doing the right thing, hard as it may be, is your Dharma.

In India, there was once a *Chipko* movement. *Chipko* literally means to cling. The movement was started in 1973 for the protection and conservation of trees by the intensity of a single individual.

After reckless felling of trees, a notable activist, Mr. Sunder Lal Bahuguna, started this movement. A large number of women from villages around would come and hold their hands around tree trunks, the larger the tree the larger the number of women around it! This prevented the tree cutters from chopping the tree down.

Eventually, an appeal from Bahuguna to Indira Gandhi, the then Prime Minister of India, resulted in a new law in 1980 banning the cutting down of trees for 25 years.

Many others have taken up causes covering areas such as Environment, Climate, Conservation, Pollution, Fauna & Flora, endangered species.

The cost-benefit dilemma in development

There are two dimensions to this. What we end up doing or not doing collectively and what we end up doing or not doing individually.

On the macro scale, there are entities like governments, industry trends, technologies deployed, collective mindsets, imperatives to improve living conditions and quality of life of the human population on this planet.

The exploitation of natural resources, large infrastructure projects, national imperatives in seeking the lowest monetary investment but having a higher damaging impact on the environment and with these the relentless growing demands for products and services. All in opposing directions to preservation and protection. It is a complex dilemma and a huge concern with no easy answers.

Collectively the human race veers towards Adharma towards the 7th circle.

Having said that even by what is in *7CircleDharma*, these issues may appear to reside in the outermost fringes of your duty towards others or other aspects. But this may well be an illusion so a balance is called for, as we have seen the consequences can walk into our inner circles very quickly.

A very few of us may be in those positions of human governance that we can dictate policy or laws. Not forgetting that the current structures and situations evolved over a large period of time where there was zero concern for the 7th circle and dismantling seems least possible. Dismantling can also be hugely disruptive to the economy and the ways of living we have become used to.

Apart from authoritarian government structures, the democratic structures of human governance do not lend themselves to generating unanimity and consensus. On a planet earth scale too, we do not have any mechanisms that can issue edicts across the planet.

Even consensus reached, maybe partial, is prone to collapse as we have seen in the Paris Climate accord. The ideas and thinking of one individual withdrew an entire most impacting country from the accord, luckily this has now been reversed. Sometimes it may not be a single person who decides, it may be the collective decision of a government.

The three gorges dam is an example. The decision to flush out radioactive water into the oceans from an impacted nuclear power plant is another.

It is easy to pick holes in what others are doing. The imperatives always trace back to the mantle of supremacy the human race has worn, still wears and will continue to wear. No easy answers. The urge the comfort zone has towards the status quo over the difficulty to battle out solutions prevails.

When this primacy of humans on the planet is taken as the root cause, there appear limited choices on what alternatives exist. If some exist there is a paucity of some resource, money, time, technology and suchlike.

Yet some progress does happen in bits and pieces. Moving away, for example, from fossil fuels into non-conventional energy sources is an effort that has gained much traction.

In India for example a huge push by Narendra Modi for non-conventional energy has started yielding result. The non-conventional sources now account for 36% of the total electricity generation capacity and this is slated to increase from the current 136 GW to 220GW by 2022. Obviously, this has displaced the power supply from fossil fuel burning power plants in a significant way.

Similarly, the global push towards electric vehicles is another such move.

These are the kind of aspects that need collective governmental will and action.

So what does one do as an individual? Each one of us will be in a unique situation, with unique needs based on your circumstance. Yet many things can be done in personal actions. To each one of us, there are some things to be mindful of.

Dharam: do not abet anyone doing damage.

Dharam: do what you can to prevent damage.

Dharam: do what you can to minimise damage.

Dharam: do what you can to repair the damage.

You can also make others aware that they do not cause damage. You can also motivate others to their duty to the 7th circle.

Many people have taken upon causes concerning protecting the planet. They have the courage of their convictions and mean well.

Sometimes however they too can move to extremes where their 7th circle concerns directly impact the inner circle concerns of individuals. While one appreciates their thoughts to bring to a standstill some ongoing or projected thing that will cause damage, the solutions really lie in the direction of finding viable alternatives.

There is and will remain a conflict between homo sapiens and the 7th circle and our Dharam is to minimise the damage.

Most of us live our lives for the present, and not have great concern for what will happen 50 or 100 years down the road.

The Indian Constitution has a section on Fundamental Duties, it says:

"It shall be the duty of every citizen of India to protect and improve the natural environment including forests, lakes, rivers and wildlife, and to have compassion for living creatures."

Acta non Verba!

CHAPTER 9

MEANWHILE... **DEEPER INSIDE YOU; THE BATTLE OF ID**

To conquer oneself is a greater victory than
to conquer thousands in a battle
~Dalai Lama

Everything that you act upon in life has a deep connect to who you are inside.

When you were born you came to this world with a clean slate, you could not think, you did not have any words let alone any concepts in your mind, incapable of language, thoughts, words – nothing programmed in your brain!

As per Lock's white paper, ' we are born with a clean slate and zero ideas in our minds...'

Yet some sort of operating system existed. Part of it was instinct, intuitive to some biological pull. A new born suckles for milk and no one teaches really. The urges within you triggered by some biological stimulus, you felt hunger (and at that time had no name for it, just some feeling), you could breathe in and out. The absence of satiation made you cry out for fulfilment. Perhaps these first need-based cries were the initial elements of communicating out that you learnt.

Slowly the brain got programmed into greater awareness levels, perhaps an inkling of day and night, wake-sleep, hunger-satiation, comfort- discomfort and a tiny seed of consciousness of your surroundings formed. Thus an ego started forming based on your increasing demands of what you wanted, as you learnt body language, then words then sentences, this started thoughts expressing clearer and clearer inside you. So you learn verbal and nonverbal language and interpret the stimuli that surround you and your mind starts to associate meaning and responses.

At this stage, your brain is still not programmed to understand abstract concepts, such as ethics, morality, justice, fairness, freedom or even god. So the first core layers of your ego are formed without any values-based relationships to your wants.

These are things that must then be learnt further. Some kind of inner understanding based on values, beliefs and culture start populating. At the initial stage, these are based on what others tell you. These are the times children ask a lot of questions as they try to relate the unknown and connect the known in some kind of growing understanding of things.

Finally, come your personal experiences and perhaps some reflection inside you as you pass through various circumstances.

The interpretations your mind makes on many abstract concepts are uniquely yours as you understand situations, perhaps at time misunderstand situations on account of their complexity or even the lack of pursuit beyond a point.

This consciousness then starts forming into your mind and

growing as a higher kind of programming and slowly coalesces into an entity within you – your ego.

But an inner core still exists within the ego, it is concerned with satiation only. This core inner self within you has been called Id by Freud. ('Id' literally 'It')

So two things exist inside you. The Ego, and within it, the Id. Now for the distinction…

The Ego is the manager inside you that controls your responses. When you say, 'I think I should do this' – that is the manager, the EGO speaking. As already mentioned, the Ego develops and continues to develop based on your conditioning and experiences.

(Do note this Ego is not synonymous to the sense we normally use the word 'egoistic')

The Id is just concerned with so-called pleasures. Satiation of some inner urges and desires. Some basal needs and instincts. It has no rationalisation mechanisms. It has no values yardstick. It has just desires for pleasurable things and fears of those not happening that operate upon it. Id has no other agendas.

The Id is happy when it experiences pleasures and creates inner turmoil to your ego (manager) when it is in a 'no pleasure' state.

The Id creates the seeking in you to fulfil and Ego seeks to focus you in the needed directions.

This then is the battle of Id, when it pulls you into arenas with no check and balance of Dharma and Adharma.

Lust, greed, and all the terms that have been called sin in contexts of different religions or unlawful things in contexts of philosophies arise from the Id and there is no way they will not, Id does not know the difference. It just can just up the want.

Your manager, the ego, has to be in full control else Id can run wild! So what really matters are who you are inside as that is your manager. Also what matters are the rules you have developed and the constructs that the manager follows.

I do not wish to set up debates on Id and Ego. These are concepts I use to bring forth a simple point.

There is an inner point within all of us that is concerned with experiencing pleasure or happiness that has no reasoning ability and no connection to any values stream.

Then beyond that is something YOU have developed into as you navigate the passage of your existence; this is the thinking you and the feeling you.

The battle between your inner desires that will pop up time and again and the way your aware self handles these is the battle of Id.

It would be obvious by now that if not well-managed Id can push you into Adharma time and again. It will well up feelings inside you, urges, as it seeks pleasure from something or the other or it seeks the freedom from fear of not having.

Homo sapiens has been on an evolutionary path and its newer versions can claim an edge because they are programmed better. Some of this started way back when the first social units were formed. One can only think in day to day matters within the boundaries of one's knowledge. Thus at different times these boundaries expanded, changed and opportunity to do things different emerged.

Having said that many times some older programming was ditched in favour of a fancy new program and regression even happened. People started refuting and recreating notions. Sometimes they get plain tired and bored and seek out new notions or trends.

As new things are discovered, new realities form and the options increase and the complexities increase.

The history of this world clearly proves that brutality was commonplace. The theme behind was coveting something and beating down the opposition physically. The theme still exists in some other form, maybe not physical. The coveting, of course, arose from the within Id.

Perhaps as religions formed, they sought to generate fear motivation to suppress the desires of Id by divine retribution. They sought to list out the good and bad, each interpretation based on the circumstance valid at that time, the key message they conveyed and convenience to their central philosophy.

Tomas Carlyle said religion is but a set of thou shalt and thou shalt nots. Ultimately many of these got codified into written laws not always connected to religion, laws with punishment.

The Old Testament talks of – the wind of human sin and the whirlwind of divine vengeance.

Thus the fear and reward combo of religions and the fear and punishment of legal statutes are external forces.

The best solution is from within, from our manager within us who is charged with the thinking behind the execution of work and perform acts. If we have a good manager within, we are better off.

Id creeps on our manager Ego in many sneaky ways. It may pop up the concept and urge to remain free. Now, this is something, 'freedom' after all is listed in positive values.

Freedom has been used curiously in two contexts.

One is that of positive freedom, i.e. free to do what you want. The other context is of negative freedom – you want to be free of prosecution. Both have impacts on how you function.

The positive freedom, do what you want must be accompanied by a limitation that it excludes negative consequences to you and to others.

The Ego manager gets disarmed at this desire to be free and if the limitation is not applied will surely progress in instances towards adharma.

Then there are stories we tell ourselves, these can create a pseudo-reality. We hate being responsible, accountable and makeup stories. A fib here and a fib there can easily grow into a bundle of untruths. So examine all stories you tell yourself and extract out the truth. That is your Dharma!

Impact of stories we tell ourselves is huge, often we are not even aware and the justifications we offer at times, created to suit an explanation, at times inventing a 'why' that was not there in the first place mixes up into a pseudo reality.

One more thought. Behind every meaning you make the roots will surely reside in your intentions. These intentions can be overt or covert. They may be hidden behind masks of pretence. Yet they represent who you are underneath all and ultimately that is what matters. Who you are is what your intentions make you out to be!

Whenever you embark on the new, take sides, review the old, seek intentions behind and they will surely tell you the real story.

Vedanta says, seek out the truth, the ultimate truth and therein you will get the proper direction.

It also says that truths are of two kinds, one is a set of truths that are absolute truths, and these remain unchanged across time, situations and places. The other truths are episodical and the intent behind, the why must be probed.

Seek the absolute truths and align thoughts and actions to those, that is your Dharma.

The best pursuits are those that are beneficial both to you and others. Seek balance, that is your Dharma.

Clearly, the only good way to live is to continuously enhance your inner manager. Yes, you have done that in the past, maybe this *7CircleDharma* too helps, yet you must get into a stage that you are continuously growing into a better and newer version. The manager must continuously build version upon version!

One way of growth comes from reflection, immediate past events, other people events, old events, stories you read. For example, if you as the simple question, what was the intent behind it, why was this done, you will find a wealth of learning. As you do this frequently you will enhance the programming of your mind to perform Dharma. Thinking 'why' is one of the most insightful exercises.

As you first why uncovers the first layer, you need to ask another why as you discover the first root cause. Till you do this to a point where the intent is uncovered you will not discover the truth.

The other area is to enhance and learn new things. Some explorations are a must, am listing some which seem important due to various reasons. Perhaps you may have started some, but when you find time to dwell on one of these with purposeful pursuit. Maybe these you could take up one by one each month and learn something of you in these contexts.

- You and your greater purposes
- You and your openness to learn
- You and your solutions
- You and your talents
- You and the stories you tell yourself
- You and your weaknesses
- You and your strengths
- You and your vision for yourself
- You and the risks you take

- You and your mindset
- You and your stability and balance during testing times

Use pen and paper and spend an hour at least to think these through. You can discover more things too beyond the above. All these will empower your inner manager.

The Id inside you is not always negative. It has the second side to the coin that can drive a person to greatness.

The key is really on which thing does the Id derive pleasure from and latch on to it.

Pleasure may come from helping others, may come when you help generate greater peace, may come when you protect the environment. Whatever gives you the sense of pleasure inside you is connected to Id.

Mahatma Gandhi, Nelson Mandela are two such examples, there would of course be many others.

Each one of us is different. What tickles you? If the Id want is aligned to a positive value and coupled with an intent to do for others, such people attain greatness and acclaim. They have found things to do without a connection to a personal material gain.

The battles in the mind erupt not always from internal agents. Many times, external stimuli trigger thoughts, some of these words or ideas you hear are extremely persuasive, influencers exist and they make demands on you to act in their directions. Sometimes they can get you into a kind of emotional blackmail, but more of this in the next chapter. At such times you may be partially moved, unmoved or swayed.

As we said earlier the why behind the ask, the intent, must always be examined. The why behind will always enlighten as you study acts you do or others do.

And keep winning the battle of Id! That is your Dharma.

CHAPTER 10

OF LOGIC & EMOTIONS
BATTLEGROUNDS OF THE MIND

At the end you should do
the right thing even if it is hard.
~ Nicholas Sparks

Any conflicts that exist must be resolved in doing your Dharma. These can arise from external circumstance or may well spring up by some inner conflict. In the end, you have to make a choice so the ultimate battleground that exists is that within your mind as you decide to act or not to act.

These are related to the manager inside you struggling to navigate alternative pulls of logic and emotions, of options arising from multiple directions, from inside and outside you all in a very dynamic environment.

There are forces at play within us based on Instinct, emotion and logic. These create waves and even tsunamis at times. Let us examine this.

When you feel hunger, it is neither emotional nor logical. It is the result of some inner biological urge. It exists in the basic level of human needs and relates to some instinctive urge within us. You may well ask how such things can impact our Dharma! For one, they prime and catalyse!

Emotions on the other hand are a state you are in as a result of some resolved or unresolved situation. Emotions wane and ebb as the inner dissatisfaction or satisfaction pushes or is pushed back or even replaced. They may last despite your logical side telling it otherwise. They may get temporarily overcome and yet persist. When they pervade and persist you get into moods. Moods are emotional states that are lasting, lingering and always based on some stimuli.

Even when you feel hungry as the body systems signals you for want of food, or thirsty due to some other biological feedback. You may 'will' it to wait and unless you have either food or water it will not leave you alone.

Similarly, you may hear some words, observe something you dislike, and some anger flares up within your mind – you feel angry. Whenever such emotion wells up it short circuits your logical brain and you get into dangerous states. Notice the trigger usually is from the outside, though can be from within you as reflection or realisation of something done pushes you. However, we are built to have our subconscious mind work from us inside pushing back and attempting to cool us down.

Anger is usually accompanied by a physical reaction within us, chemicals enter your bloodstream, your blood pounds faster feeding the angry state. The biochemical association will also wane and help you cool down. So both body and mind will work to push down the emotion, how long it takes is a different matter.

Sometimes you see the funny side of it and this displaces the anger fast and the humour based emotional state takes over. Again, you may strongly wonder what all this has to do with Dharma.

One more aspect before the dots connect!

Till now what you have read in the *7CircleDharma*, its methodology, is concerned with the logical state of mind. The calm you; observing, reflecting, remembering, relating and responding! Ideas, contexts, priorities, suggested actions – all relate to a logical sequence. They reside and appeal to logic.

These logical elements are in grave danger in highly emotional states, and it is in these emotional states that most acts of Adharma get seeded. Thereafter the logical side gets diverted into building up justifications and explanations or stories that you tell yourself and others.

What is key here is that two types of gateways exist in our mind. The emotional and logical gateways and these cause things to shift their circles.

An inanimate object, a small crystal, you see it and some greed overcomes you. Maybe your Id is saying, I would love to possess this. The object may be in your 7th circle, not your property and you suddenly get the urge to possess it. It has started moving orbits and approaching your 1st circle just by virtue of the urge-thought you got.

Now you may still have the logical gateway open and it tells you that you have to pay for it to possess it. So far so good. But then the logical mind says you don't have the money to buy. This may subdue the urge.

Then the greed inside, the Id aided by some negative thoughts conspire and you get the desire to own it at any cost, steal it, pay for it, but own it you must. The urge-desire starts opening an emotional gateway and now Dharma or Adharma can result. This is the choice point you have as you say yes or no to the urge. This is where the seed point of Dharma resides.

The crystal diamond is just an example. It can be replaced with other objects of desire and pleasure and right or wrong pathways to possess.

Emotions causing obsessive need will always cause Adharma. Primed by Id and sustained by emotional states

Another example, you see an appealing person at a party or someplace for the first time. This person is in your 6th circle. Some inner feeling, perhaps primed by some inner sexual instinct or by just a liking, urges you to attempt to meet and talk. The minute you do so this person moved into your 5th circle. In some cases, you may want just more than that and a gateway to the first circle starts opening up.

You may have met your future spouse or partner and would then get settled in your second circle admitted and facilitated in through the emotional gateway. All fine and Dharma flows.

However, many crimes are committed when lust, greed, coveting or other emotions take obsessive control, these open non-logical gateways that get to Adharma actions.

Do be cautious of the gateway of emotion. This is where despite the best of your intentions you may get captured into Adharma. Let a bit of cooling down in and get your logical mind to work, this is a good way to stay in Dharma.

Of the other gateway, the logical one, where you think through and decide purely on logic. Seems perfect and is not always so. There has to be a tempering of empathy when your logical gateways flow out to actions.

It is this empathy that makes you human and has to be woven in with positive logic.

It is emotions that can also make you a demon when they work solo or accompanied by a false negative justification seemingly of a logical nature.

Reactive behaviour will eat away the check and balance of positive values as well as your Dharma foundations.

When emotions are high, make it a point to pause then respond and not react. At the same time, one must also check for any fault lines in the logical frame.

The ones you love the most are the ones who can exert the most emotional appeal. The asks that come from them can be repeated or even nudges to move you in a certain direction. The emotional connect of love can cloud you and you may end up doing things that you really did not want to do. It has to be from your own choice and not from the emotional appeal of others.

Impulsive behaviour is another area where some action has won the day even before you examined the conflict in the mind. Impulsive action can lead you to Adharma and regret. So the pause and response is a good habit to develop.

Conflicting desires within you are one prime source of conflict. A desire not to offend versus speaking out. A desire for revenge against the desire to live in peace. The negative and positive pairs obviously will conflict. However even competing positives can produce ripples.

There may be a need to deal with a situation with discipline and some desire inside you that loves the person. A parent-child situation is one obvious situation where such a conflict may arise.

Sometimes we are doing things that are all right to do but suddenly we get engaged in some kind of race or contest and the desire to win overextends the quantum beyond a permissible limit. These races we run get us into mindless patterns of existence and a madness of pursuit. To win at any cost – then the cost usually is of Dharma.

Many conflicts arise because of the clash of some values. Some of these may be based on philosophies we subscribe to. Service to others is a positive value, and when this happens at the cost of denial to some inner circle the conflict is obvious. Follow the circle priorities is a good way out.

People can make demands, influence you, convince you to entertain a line of thought. Once you start deliberating or deciding on these conflict can get set up primarily of what you perceive as expectations you must fulfil. To be or not to be!

Thus the battles can be set up from inside or outside of you. Several situations trigger:

- People cajoling you
- People influencing you with logic or emotion
- People ordering you, or demanding
- Repeated asks
- Asks that you respond to impulsively
- People challenging you
- People enticing you
- People criticising you to get reaction
- Suggestions
- Telling you stuff
- Copying others
- Things you come across that seem interesting or appealing
- Media planting ideas in your head

All these and more can set up conflicts primed by the external environment and as soon as you start debating to do or not to do the conflict, the battle is on.

Another source is the clash of ideologies. For example, in socialist societies, it is common to have actions that will provide the benefit to all citizens, broad base the impact of whatever is being done. On the other hand, this may clash with the freedom to work for your own benefit. Thus, helping others versus helping yourself sets up conflicts. Many political, religious and other ways of thinking can produce huge conflicts.

Similarly, there is a clash between cultures. There may be clashes arising out of differing interests. Differing generations and what they hold dear can trigger conflict. In fact, the change that is always happening will polarise the old versus the new.

Reaching down to the absolute truths, the root causes and intentions can help you vastly in managing yourself in many types of conflicts. This of course then needs to be accompanied by subsequent right action.

One must always be careful when we set goals, as these precede actions. Having the conflicts resolved at that stage prevents you from commitment to arising conflicts. The goals you set should also stand the test of Dharma.

The first layer to tackle is always to manage the emotion. Then the second layer, the gateway of the logical mind will open. Then the solution can usually be found using the *7CircleDharma* as a guideline.

Managing your emotions is your Dharma.

CHAPTER 11

BEYOND ALL THIS
WHERE DOES GOD FIT IN?

Whence all creation had its origin,
the creator, whether he fashioned it
or whether he did not, the creator,
who surveys it all from highest heaven,
he knows — or maybe even he does not know.
~ Rigveda Samhita

Vivekananda says; The two great divisions of the Vedas are Karam Kanda – the portion pertaining to doing or work, and the Jnana Kanda – the portion related to knowing, true knowledge.

The Karam Yogi wants everyone to be saved before himself. The Jnana Kanda teaches us that knowledge alone can save... become wise unto salvation.

The Greeks started a train of thought, that a person must be respected not just as an instrument of an omnipotent overlord, but for his own sake. Pericles said. 'Each single one of our citizens, in all the manifold aspects of life, is able to show himself the rightful lord and owner of his own person, and to do this moreover with exceptional grace and exceptional versatility. This then was their description of Liberty and how the individual must come across.

Is there something beyond this?

Perhaps beyond the positive values we have of any kind, may exist a spiritual zone or connect. The exploration of this book is to the point of values and whatever that represent pinnacles of ultimate truths. What lies beyond I leave to you and to the many religious scholars as they relate and explain the edicts that contain surely many positive values.

So for people who seek to know where does God fit in, to each one what he or she thinks, do surely connect beyond the realm of positive values into whatever spiritual domain that you have faith in.

This *7CircleDharma* is about the present, your action or inaction, the reasons behind such, the principles you use to decide, the consequences you generate and the degree of happiness you can generate within yourself and others.

The meaning of the word *Veda*, is knowledge. Truths that stay intact across time, space and causation. So what we do in our life to do our Dharma in this context. Your intent, your values, your duties, your purposes, your behaviour and your actions are what primarily concern the *7CircleDharma* practices. As I mentioned behind the values you pursue may exist a spiritual domain if you so believe.

The connect to God is a different exploration best left to the ones who are experts in that domain!

Am ending this chapter with something to dwell upon, from Swami Vivekananda's poem:

No one to blame

The sun goes down, its crimson rays
Light up the dying day,
A startled glance I throw behind
And count my triumph shame;
    No one but me to blame

Each day my life I make or mar,
Each deed begets its kind,
Good good, bad bad, the tide once set
No one can stop or stem;
    No one but me to blame

I am my own embodied past;
Therein the plan was made;
The will, the thought, to that conform,
To that the outer frame;
    No one but me to blame

Love comes reflected back as love
Hate breeds more fierce hate
They mete their measures, lay on me
Through life and death their claim;
    No one but me to blame

I cast off fear and vain remorse
I feel my Karma's sway
I face the ghosts my deeds have raised –
Joy, sorrow, censure, fame;
    No one but me to blame

Good, bad, love, hate and pleasure, pain
Forever linked go,
I dream of pleasure without pain,
It never, never came
No one but me to blame

I give up hate, I give up love,
My thirst for life is gone;
Eternal death is what I want,
Nirvanam goes life's flame;
No one is left to blame

Meantime, you have to continue living and wish you all the best to do your Dharma.

AND NOW, DO YOUR DHARMA!

www.ingramcontent.com/pod-product-compliance
Ingram Content Group UK Ltd.
Pitfield, Milton Keynes, MK11 3LW, UK
UKHW041823200726
13854UKWH00002BA/512